# FAITH AND REASON

# FAITH AND REASON

A *Comparative Study of Pascal, Bergson and James*

By

JAMES DEOTIS ROBERTS

THE CHRISTOPHER PUBLISHING HOUSE
BOSTON, U.S.A.

COPYRIGHT © 1962
BY THE CHRISTOPHER PUBLISHING HOUSE

*Library of Congress Catalog Card Number 62-12276*

PRINTED IN
THE UNITED STATES OF AMERICA

DEDICATED

TO

MY WIFE, ELIZABETH; MY DAUGHTER, CHARMAINE

AND MY SON, DEOTIS, JR.

# PREFACE

The problem of faith and reason is contemporary; for it keeps ever before us ultimate questions and the values of time and eternity. The problem is, what is the rapport of faith and reason in the search for truth and reality?

The aim of this study is to compare what Pascal, Bergson and James have to say about the problem of faith and reason. This problem has been for the author a live issue for some time and for this reason this study has been of great interest in the clarification of his thought. Dorothy Eastwood, in her *Revival of Pascal*, has stated that Bergson and James are responsible in part for the recent revival of interest in the thought of Pascal. Accordingly, the author considers her book a very valuable one in this study, especially in comparing the basic presuppositions of the men here being studied. It is the author's opinion that the agreement between them is basic though not organic in the sense that a definite line of development may be traced from Pascal to the others.

There is a further observation, viz. that the philosophical climates of the philosophers of this study reveal a remarkable similarity and that attitudes toward their various backgrounds are also similar. They make a radical break from the position to which they object (the autonomy of the rational method) and swing to the opposite view (the affirmation of intuition). The "reasons of the heart" of Pascal are basic to all three philosophers. We shall attempt to show, however, that each has his own metaphysical framework in developing his notion of immediate apprehension of truth, and thus the differences are as pronounced as the similarities.

In this study I am endeavoring to compare the views of Bergson and James with that of Pascal; for it is my candid opinion that Pascal's view is the more reasonable and is supported by Christian thought. The attempt will be made to substantiate this claim by using Pascal as a standard of judgment throughout this study.

The author is indebted to R. G. Collingwood for the method used in this study, i.e., the denial and affirmation of philosophical positions both as applied to the philosophers whose thought is used in this study and to the treatment given to the problem in the following pages.[1] All true philosophers are influenced by their predecessors, directly or indirectly, positively or negatively, and, as Collingwood declares, the philosopher knows what he denies and what he affirms at once.

The plan of this study is as follows:

Chapter I will examine the discovery by Pascal, Bergson and James of the limitations of rational knowledge. Chapter II will be concerned with the affirmations of these philosophers as to the nature of faith or supra-rational knowledge (to be used as synonyms in this study). Chapter III will evaluate the findings of previous chapters and the conclusion will attempt to draw out the implications that have been discovered in this study.

The author is grateful to Prof. William L. Bradley for his guidance as advisor of this study; to Prof.

## PREFACE

Ford Battles for many stylistic suggestions; to Mrs. Anna M. Nesbitt for her services as typist; to my family for their long-suffering and to all others who made this study possible.

J. DEOTIS ROBERTS

*Washington, D.C.*
*1961*

# TABLE OF CONTENTS

Preface ............................................................. vii

I. The Discovery of the Limits of Rational Knowledge ........................................ 13
    A. Introductory ............................................ 13
    B. The Development of Pascal's Thought ................................... 15
    C. Why Bergson Arrives at His Theory of Knowledge ............................................. 24
    D. Why James Affirms the Limits of the Rational Method ..................................... 27

II. The Attainment of Supra-Rational Knowledge .......................................... 36
    A. Pascal on the Primacy of Faith ............. 37
    B. Bergson on Intuition: Open and Dynamic Manifestations ...................... 43
    C. James Views Faith and the Right-to-Believe ................................................. 50

III. Contribution to the Problem of Faith and Reason — A Critique — Conclusion ..................................................... 61
    A. Pascal as Criterion of Judgment ............ 61

## TABLE OF CONTENTS

    B. "The Reasons of the Heart" in Pascal, James and Bergson .................................. 63

    C. The Mystic Experience in Pascal, Bergson and James .................................. 67

    D. The Wager Argument of Pascal and James .......................................................... 74

    E. Conclusion ............................................... 80

Footnotes and References ................................ 85

Bibliography ....................................................... 93

Appendix ............................................................. 97

# Faith and Reason

## CHAPTER I

## THE DISCOVERY OF THE LIMITS OF RATIONAL KNOWLEDGE

### A. INTRODUCTORY

Pascal, Bergson and James agree that rational knowledge is limited. We turn now to the development of their thought, endeavoring to discover what led each of them to this conclusion. We are reminded, at the outset, of a difference among the philosophers of this study — with Pascal on one hand — and Bergson and James on the other. Pascal's discovery of the limits of rational knowledge is more subjective than the others. Once he has made the discovery he gives a great deal of effort to establish the reasons for his objection to the autonomy of the rational method. Accordingly, we may receive from his own writings a clear statement as to why he drew his conclusion. It is likewise to be understood that Pascal treats specifically the problem of faith and reason in his *Apology* and that it is the strategy of this work to compare the two ways of knowing that we might choose the better. When we turn to Bergson and James we are not so fortunate, for their approach is more objective and they never feel the conflict which Pascal experiences. They seek truth but they develop a theory of knowledge for this purpose. When they turn to experience they do so mainly because concepts have failed them. The problem of faith and reason is implied in their writings but it is not central. Accordingly, we understand why they admit the limits of rational knowledge primarily from the development of their thought. The fact is that after discovering the limits of the rational method they spend most of their efforts in developing the new position and what they have to say concerning faith is the application of their new theory rather than its central theme. With this in mind, we shall take a look at their philosophical climate, observe some problems which cast light upon their affirmation that rationality is finite and attempt to draw some inferences from their writing which give the reasons for their conclusions. Bergson and James know, almost from the beginning, for what they seek, and they look in various directions until they find an answer in intuition. On the other side of the account Pascal appears not to know what he is seeking at first, and seeks at random. The dawning comes when he begins his study of man, but his real insight, as to what he seeks, comes with his Second Conversion. Subsequently he knows what his previous search has been and the answer to this quest. His *Pensées* point in both directions and this makes clear the comparison of faith with discursive reason. Pascal's unique insight is due not to what he found himself as much as to what God reveals to him by the illumination of Grace. We have in Pascal's *Pensées* a personal testimony which speaks of this knowledge of faith and the limits of the rational method. For this reason, Pascal has a standard of

## FAITH AND REASON

judgment which the others do not have, namely the fact of the Incarnation.[1] We turn now to the influences which led Pascal to affirm the finitude of reason.

### B. The Development of Pascal's Thought

First, let us observe the scientific influences behind the thought of Pascal. There were several scientific methods employed in Pascal's time: There was the Aristotelian, which had a rationalistic and metaphysical approach to physical science. Then there was the purely empirical approach of the alchemists, with Bacon as their master, which disdained philosophy and mathematics. There were also the astrologers with a panpsychic theory of the universe. Finally, there was the geometrical method, which dealt with the physical world on the basis of its component factors of movement, number, and space. This latter type was divided on metaphysics. Galileo defined the substance of material things in terms of extension; Gassendi had an atomic theory of the universe, his atoms being indivisible material corpuscles. All its adherents, however, agree that the task of science was to reduce physical phenomena to quantities which could be measured and counted.[2] Pascal was influenced by the geometrical approach, which adhered to the method of Galileo. He found the greatest possible freedom of purely scientific thought and action in employing this method.[3]

According to Patrick, Pascal's *theorem* on the properties of conic sections contained the germ of his entire method of understanding mathematics, that is to say, that the properties of a complex figure may be considered as modifications and resemblances of a simpler figure. Here we find the Platonic idea of participation, according to which all things are an image or an imitation of ideas;[4] and from it we gain an inkling of the Pascalian doctrine of orders, which sees in art an imitation of a natural model, in the world of morals the imitation of a supernatural model, God, and in nature a symbol, or a distorted image, of Grace.[5]

Pascal insists that outside of geometry there are no real demonstrations and that apart from axioms, which are principles springing from a direct apprehension of truth, and deductions, there is no scientific certainty.[6] He also states that experiment must be followed in physics.[7] Thus his axioms are related to the world of ideal essences.[8]

The way of truth is not direct; it is the way of negation. It is natural for man to believe that he possesses the truth directly; and he is always disposed to deny all that is incomprehensible to him; whereas the only thing he knows is falsehood and he must accept as true only those things whose opposites appear false to him. This is why every time a proposition is inconceivable, it is necessary to suspend judgment about it and not deny it for that reason, but examine its opposite; and if one finds that to be false, one may affirm the former.

Patrick places Pascal in the history of science midway between Descartes and Bacon, higher than either, but not as high as Galileo.[9] Descartes sought to deduce all the sciences from some clear and distinct ideas; but Pascal asserted that experiments are the only guides in metaphysics. Pascal was influenced by Descartes in overstressing deduction in his theory of scientific method. Bacon was almost exclusively an empiricist,

## FAITH AND REASON

relying on experiments and induction, not realizing the importance of stating natural laws in mathematical form. On the other hand, Pascal reduced his results to statements of general principle. Accordingly, Pascal took up the opposite qualities of those two pioneers into the higher synthesis of his genius; and this is perhaps what led him to the notion of the two contrary truths: "all their principles are true. . . . But their conclusions are false, because the opposite principles are true also."[10] Pascal comes close to Galileo, for both use experiment and reduce physical problems to mathematical terms. Galileo, however, is superior to Pascal in scientific theory. Galileo considers scientific induction as useful and necessary and leaves room for imagination in the formulation of scientific hypotheses. Pascal, on the contrary, is unduly cautious and conservative at this point.[11] In the search for truth, the latter discovers the unity and relations of things which appear widely separated.

Pascal is led by his own method to the same problem with which Descartes had already struggled. Pascal begins his search by stating that the perfect method consists in employing no term without first clearly explaining its meaning, and in advancing no proposition without demonstrating it by known truths. This is impossible as it involves an infinite regress. Thus, men do not have the perfect method at their disposal. Geometry comes as close to it as possible; it defines everything except things which are known by all and presupposes that everyone knows what is meant by such primary concepts as movement, number, and space.[12]

Movement, number, and space are reciprocally related. Movement cannot be conceived apart from motion and is one with it; this relation of movement with the thing moved is the unity behind the origin of all numbers. Movement is related to space, and all three — movement, number and space — are interwoven. Time, likewise, is included; for movement and time are related. Accordingly, Pascal asserts that there are properties common to all things, the knowledge of which opens one's mind in wonder as he looks at nature.[13]

Pascal is acquainted with the geometry of chance, which is revealed in his later thought. He solves the problem of dividing stakes in an unfinished game of chance and develops a system of analysis based on combinations. The basic principles of his work in this field he applies to the problem of deciding for or against the existence of God.[14]

The result of the scientific preoccupations of Pascal is his discovery that they do not help understand the human heart or the ultimate questions derived from the mystery of the universe and human destiny. After spending much time in the abstract sciences, Pascal becomes disgusted.

> Turning to the study of man, I saw that these abstract sciences are alien to man, and that plunging into them I was wandering further from my proper condition than others who had no knowledge of them. I forgave them their ignorance; but I thought at least to find many companions in the study of mankind, which is man's proper study. . . . It is only from not knowing how to study man that we go after other things; but is it not true that they do not contain the knowledge man ought to have, and that, if he would be happy, he had better remain in ignorance of himself?[15]

This leads him to philosophy, searching for truth untouched by mathematics. He becomes interested in the writings of Epictetus and Montaigne. The former,

## FAITH AND REASON

Epictetus, viewed the universe as the work of God, the spirit of God as the soul of the universe, and man as a part of the universe who ought to unite himself by reason and will to the life of the universe. He said he had never been prevented from doing what he wanted to do or compelled to do the opposite. He found happiness by cooperating with the inevitable, i.e., making one's desires coincide with what is in one's power and being indifferent to all else. Pascal is tormented by his inability to regulate his heart and cannot accept this superficial optimism. "Epictetus knew perfectly the way," says Pascal, "and he told men their way was false. He tells them of another way, but he does not lead there."[16]

On the other hand, Pascal finds a corrective in Montaigne and considers his writings valuable. Montaigne insisted that man cannot grasp the ultimate nature of things or find a rule of conduct in reason alone. His view that everything is in perpetual flux corresponds with the insight of geometry into the incessant movement of quantities between the incomprehensible infinities. But when Pascal looks to Montaigne for some guiding principle for a practical life, what he finds is a doctrine which is too easy and shallow to bring him satisfaction. "The faults of Montaigne," says Pascal, "are many."[17] "What Montaigne said is untrue to the facts of life.[18] Both Epictetus and Montaigne evade the vital principle of our life." According to Pascal, "despite the sight of all our miseries, which touch us . . . we have an instinct which raises us up."[19]

By way of comparison, Epictetus exalts us to look to God and see our likeness and he tells us to adore God, for we are created to be like Him. He reminds us of our greatness as men. On the other hand, Montaigne says, "Look down to the earth, puny as you are and observe the beasts, your companions."[20] He reminds us of our misery. Pascal raises the questions: What is man? Is he equal to God or to beasts? He concludes that man is lost and he has fallen from the place where he once knew rest.[21] Accordingly, Epictetus and Montaigne present two points of view which Pascal considers important. Either one believes that God is the sovereign good or one is uncertain and incapable of the goodness of God.

These viewpoints are false according to Pascal, for they do not recognize the fact that man has changed since he was created. Epictetus considers only the greatness of man, being ignorant of his corruption. On the other side of the account, Montaigne believes in man's misery and ignores his dignity. The former view leads to pride while the latter creates despair and indifference. Man, according to Pascal, must know his greatness and misery together for his own good. The paradox appears when they are united. The proper study of these authors should prove valuable. Epictetus may disturb those who seek rest in external things alone and make them aware of their misery and error without God. On the other hand, Montaigne may confound pride among those who consider themselves as being truly just without faith. Faith, according to Pascal, leads one to forsake a dogmatic view of both science and philosophy for a higher truth.

Pascal discovers that factors other than clearness and distinctness (Descartes) must be considered if man is to have true knowledge. Accordingly, it is through his Second Conversion that he realizes that the relationship of man to God is the basis of genuine knowledge. His personal affirmation of faith is the key to the understanding of his *Apology*. The views

# FAITH AND REASON

of Epictetus and Montaigne cancel each other to give way to the Gospel. The way to reconcile the contrary truths found in his two favorite authors, concludes Pascal, is to affirm both. He seeks to find a higher truth to harmonize them in one synthesis and through his Second Conversion he finds the higher truth, the Incarnation.[22]

Through this religious experience, Pascal realizes the futility of mere intellectual proofs for the existence of God. He speaks of knowing that God exists by the feelings of the heart.[23] For this purpose, he urges men to search their hearts and observe the truth of what God speaks. Here alone does one know of the order of faith and love. In that order, the irreconcilable contradictions are held together; the reason for them becomes clear; their reconciliation by God is disclosed.[24] Thus the culmination of Pascal's quest is not in mathematics or philosophy but in his mystic experience through which he realized inner peace.

Patrick has observed:

> The quest of Pascal for truth, for real knowledge became a reality to him through his Second Conversion. This event crowned his search. It is, "immediate apprehension, *Dieu sensible au coeur, non à la raison*," which brought him peace of soul.[25]

By way of conclusion, Pascal discovers that no human science can be exact and that the human mind is finite and unable to comprehend the infinite and the eternal. Nevertheless, man is formed for truth even if he cannot reach true knowledge by rational means. Hence, Pascal suggests that man study nature well and at the same time study himself to recognize what his place is in nature and by so doing he will recognize his smallness. Nature is infinite in scope, her center is everywhere, her circumference nowhere.[26]

Man should be aroused to a consideration of what he is when compared with the reality of things. "What is a man face to face with infinity?"[27] On the other hand, let him seek out the smallest thing he knows, and when by examination he concludes that he has reached the limit of minuteness in Nature, he will be amazed by the infinitely small as well as by the infinitely large. Pascal says:

> I will open to him an abyss. I will paint for him not only the visible universe, but all the imaginable vastness of Nature enclosed within this atomized atom. Let him behold there an infinity of universes, each with its firmament, planets, earth in the same proportion as the visible world or living creatures on the earth, and finally mites in which I will find again all that was in the first and still finding in the rest the same repeated endlessly, ceaselessly; let him stand dumb before these wonders as amazing in their minuteness as the others in their vastness. For who can fail to marvel that our human body, which anon was imperceptible in the sum of things, is now a colossus, nay a void, nay a universe, compared with the nothingness which lies beyond our reach?[28]

Let man gaze at these infinities and he will be terrified; for he will realize that he is suspended between two abysses of Infinity and Nothingness. Upon beholding these wonders, one should marvel and gaze in silence, rather than assert the sufficiency of his mind to grasp them.[29]

> Man is a mean between zero and all. He is unable to grasp these extremes. First principles are hidden from him. He is unable to answer the questions of *whence* and *whither*. He gets, at best, only a glimpse of the mean of things. His lot is despair. The author of these wonders comprehends them, no other can.[30]

And thus Pascal admonishes us to know our limits and realize that we are something, but not all. Our intelligence, like our bodies, is a mean between two extremes and this middle state figures in all our faculties. This is our condition, which renders us incapable

# FAITH AND REASON

of certain knowledge or absolute ignorance. Our reason is ever cheated by misleading appearances. Accordingly, in the face of these infinities all finites are equal.[31]

> ... What completes our capacity to know things is the fact that they are simple in themselves, whereas we are composed of two natures, viz. soul and body. It is impossible for the reasoning part in us to be other than spiritual ... (matter cannot know itself).... If we are simply material, we can know nothing at all, and if we are composed of spirit and matter we cannot know perfectly things that are simple, whether spiritual or corporeal. Most philosophers confound ideas and speak of matter in spiritual terms and of spiritual things in terms of matter.... Man is to himself the most abnormal object in Nature, for he cannot conceive what his body is, and least of all how a body can be united to a mind. This is man's crowning difficulty, and yet it is his essential being. *How the spirit is attached to the body is incomprehensible to man, and yet this is what man is.*[32]

Pascal reminds us of our finitude and urges us to self-examination that we may find true knowledge as well as our proper relation to God. Man needs to find God, according to Pascal, for in Him all truth is found. Rational knowledge cannot prove the existence of God, for the last step it can take is the recognition of the infinity which lies beyond.[33]

> I will show you something which is infinite and indivisible: A point moving in every direction with infinite rapidity, for it is everywhere and is complete in every place. This natural phenomenon, which hitherto seemed to you impossible, may perhaps teach you that there may be others which as yet you do not know. *Do not draw the conclusion from your apprenticeship that there is nothing left for you to learn, but rather that there remains an infinity of things to know.*[34]

We see from this that Pascal sets forth clearly the reason he considers rational knowledge as finite. Much of the same conclusion is found in the writings of Bergson, whose thought is to be examined next.

### C. Why Bergson Arrives At His Theory of Knowledge

First, we observe the philosophical milieu of Bergson to understand the stimulations behind his affirmations. He reckons with the philosophy of Mill and Spencer, who view man as a mere automaton. This positivistic empiricism receives the support of a metaphysic which considers man as the measure of all things. The absolute idealism of Hegel, whose thought is linked with pantheism similar to that of Spinoza, makes the universe a necessary corollary to mind and man is inserted in the place of God. Accordingly, human intelligence becomes the absolute measure of the intelligible, by identifying itself with the mind which thinks and necessarily produces the world. This mixture of determinism and pantheistic idealism ends in monism. Positivism (under the influence of Hume), denied the metaphysical and became entrenched in the human order. Comte is an example of a philosopher who employs positivistic methods. Bergson reacts against the above theories of knowledge.

There was, however, another current of thought in France at the beginning of the twentieth century, under the influence of the philosophy of Maine de Biran, which considered the human mind capable of reaching the absolute and making it the object of speculation. This metaphysic found its roots in the depths of the inner life. Ravaisson, Lachelier and Boutroux represent this trend of thought, and they lay a foundation for Bergson's thought. Material idealism is displaced by a spiritual realism in these philosophers. Accordingly, Bergson rejects positivism and turns away from German idealists and from Kant. On the other side of the account, he is in some respects the successor of Boutroux as well as of Ravaisson and Lachelier, and the more advanced his thought becomes the closer he approximates that of Maine de Biran and Pascal.[35]

To be more specific as to why Bergson arrives at his conclusion that the rational method is limited, we observe his treatment of the problem of time. Bergson was stimulated by Spencer, but when he was faced with the problem of time as duration he abandoned Spencer's method, for he rejected the materialistic and mathematical space-time for a time known by experience. Bergson concludes that mechanical facts are unable to present the real and thus he turns to the inner life to make contact with the facts of experience. Accordingly, Bergson affirms the limits of the rational method.[36] The inner life, according to Bergson, is known by duration and is characterized by flux, continuity, indivisibility and creativity.

Where Bergson desires to seek reality, namely at its source, rational concepts will not lead him. Upon facing new problems Bergson keeps in mind his purpose and for this reason continuous growth may be observed in his thought. The pattern of this development is as follows: the fact of liberty, 1889; the reality of the spirit, 1897; creation as a fact, 1907; the love which causes all, God, 1932.[37]

Bergson disproves the theory that the brain is the seat of conscious life. This is another demonstration of the reason why he considers discursive reason as finite. He is opposed to the dualism of subject-object in perception and insists on the relation between the brain and the mind.[38] According to Bergson, memory conserves itself in an unconsciousness which is part of our experience and he bases his metaphysics upon experience, which he considers as transcending concepts and simple logic. It is, then, in the very nature of the problems Bergson treats and the method he employs that he finds the rational method inadequate. Bergson seeks to establish the primacy of mind over matter and finds that concepts materialize spiritual notions; this he will not have. Accordingly, he abandons the ready-made concepts which intellectualism considers as fixed for a pliable philosophy modeling itself on a reality which is moving. According to Bergson, our faculty of intuition rules on this reality and truth also.[39]

In this respect Péguy says of Bergson:

"The denunciation of a universal intellectualism, or a universal weakness consisting of the constant following of ready-made concepts is the foundation of the philosophy of Bergson"[40]

Péguy continues by insisting that Bergson never was irrational or anti-rational and that he liberates philosophy from the rigid systems of intellectualism, like materialism and positivism. Bergson considers these metaphysics as willful destroyers of the advance of knowledge.[41]

The shortcomings of intellectualism are apparent to Bergson and intellect is assigned by him the role of an instrument of action. For the purpose of action it is necessary to specify and fix some present aspect of the environment, and the object of action must be held by attention. Through the repetition of such attitudes the intellect elaborates a scheme or diagram in which the several terms of analysis are correlated. These, in turn, remain distinct and external, but are woven by relations into a system, which is like its component terms in being stereotyped. The intellect, according to Bergson, cannot correct itself; for the further it proceeds the more thoroughly does it reduce reality to this form.

# FAITH AND REASON

It is this form itself, and not any specific phase of it, that is foreign to reality. Bergson concludes, for this reason, that reality cannot be known by the rational method. Reality abides in fluidity rather than fixity; it abides in continuity; not in space, but in time defined as pure duration. The intellect spatializes time, conceiving it as a linear series of instants, but real time cannot be known in this manner; for it is a continuous and cumulative history. Accordingly, real time is not thought but lived because it transcends intellect.

William James reminds us that Bergson came into metaphysics by way of mathematics and that it was the problem of time which stimulated him.[42] We know that the psychological principle of the unconscious influenced him greatly; for it is reflected in his notions of duration, the *élan vital*, and the general assertion that the principle of life is spiritual. Anyone who arrives at the presuppositions that Bergson does must agree that intellectualism is not the answer. Viewing the problems of time, liberty, mind and life itself from the viewpoint of Bergson, it is immediately apparent that discursive reason is finite. Accordingly, Bergson tells us that if we seek the essence of reality our method must be something other than that of intellectualism, and of course he recommends the method of intuition. A similar conclusion is drawn by James, as we shall soon see.

### D. Why James Affirms The Limits Of The Rational Method

In observing the growth of the thought of James, we discover why he recognizes the limits of the rational method. In science he goes to facts; in psychology he is concerned with the continuity of experience and the subliminal self, both of which evade rational treatment; and when he turns to morality and religion he realizes that life is more than logic.

Under Agassiz, James studied natural science, and through his motivation James was taught to look at the facts.[43] James says of Agassiz:

"The hours I spent with Agassiz so taught me the difference between all possible abstractionists and livers in the light of the world of concrete fullness, that I have never been able to forget."[44]

James derived from his study of natural science with Agassiz one distinction which remained with him, viz. the point that it is time for philosophy to abandon the path of intellectualism and logical dogmatism to imitate the sciences in going beyond to the foundation of particular facts. He is greatly concerned with the distinction between abstract and concrete thinking.[45]

James weighs the validity of theoretical speculation and its relation to concrete experience. All our ideas, hypotheses, and doctrines, in short, everything that is thought as opposed to that which is perceived, indicate a short cut evading immediately experienced facts.[46]

As a corollary to this position James rejects monistic determinism.[47] He does not accept the notion of the absolute unity of all existence. When one admits that there is but one sole reality, whose empirical variety is only a delusive appearance of a temporal unfolding, much is lost. Our personalities lose their value, and life its meaning. Furthermore, monistic systems are founded upon insufficient evidence, in fact, upon intellectualism. They fail to account for empirical data which contradict their position. In beginning this protest against monism, James finds the writings of Renouvier very helpful. He comments:

# FAITH AND REASON

". . . But for the decisive impression made upon me by Renouvier's masterly advocacy of pluralism, I might never have got free from the monistic superstition under which I had grown up."[48]

The two kinds of monism which James was most occupied in opposing were the authoritative philosophies of the time. These were forms of pantheistic idealism, represented on the one hand by the Hegelian or absolutist school of Oxford (Green, Cairds, Bradley), and on the other by Royce.[49] Against these James opposed a pluralistic philosophy of pure experience. Tychism, Pluralism, Pure Experience, Radical Empiricism, Theism and Meliorism are terms used by James to describe his philosophy. According to Flournoy, the most appropriate word to describe the philosophy of James is tychism, meaning *chance*.[50]

In the writings of James intellectualism is charged with a blind and excessive use of concepts. Concepts are fixed while sense and feeling are in flux. We may have conceptual truth *about* a thing; this is truth so far as it goes, but James declares that this is not far enough. Accordingly, the world is not known by one concept of it; for it has many aspects and relations which may be known only by intuition. It is false to assume that because a thing has one definable character, it cannot also have others; and that because it has been named first for one of its aspects, the others must be reduced or deduced from it. The error of intellectualism lies in the misuse of concepts, and not in the nature of concepts themselves. To go beyond concepts is not to *add* more concepts but to abandon them for the immediate apprehension of reality. Accordingly, James offers to us his pragmatic method, which bases its formulations on experience rather than concepts. By observation of the presuppositions of pragmatism, as James views it, we understand the trend of his thought.

Paul Tillich has well said:

> Pragmatism, as developed by William James . . . reveals the philosophical motive behind this elevation of experience to the highest ontological rank, viz. Reality is identified with experience. The motive is to deny the split between an ontological subject and ontological objects, for, once established, this split cannot be overcome, the possibility of knowledge cannot be explained and the unity of life and its processes remains a mystery.[51]

As James has said, metaphysics inquires into the cause, the substance, the meaning and the outcome of all things.

> The principles of explanation that underlie all things without exception, the elements common to all gods and men and animals and stones, the first *whence* and the last *whither* of the whole cosmic procession, the conditions of all knowing, the most general rules of human action; these furnish the problems commonly deemed philosophic *par excellence;* and the philosopher is the man who finds the most to say about them.[52]

With this notion of philosophy in mind, James faces the dilemma (of rationalism and empiricism). Rationalists are men of principles, while empiricists are men of facts. Principles are universals and facts are particulars. Accordingly, rationalists proceed from wholes to parts, while empiricists proceed from parts to wholes. Rationalists prefer to deduce facts from principles; on the contrary, empiricists prefer to explain principles as deductions from facts. Aristotle, the Scholastics, Descartes, Spinoza, Leibnitz, Kant, and Hegel are examples of the claim to absolute finality for their systems. On the other hand, empiricism strives to keep more in touch with actual life. Socrates, Locke, Berkley, Hume, Mill, Lange, Dewey, Schiller and

# FAITH AND REASON

Bergson are examples of this type. Kant's thought and that of Royce is a mixture of rationalism and empiricism.[53] James confesses: "The author of this volume is weakly endowed on the rationalist side, and his book will show a strong leaning toward empiricism."[54]

Among the intellectualists two parties may be distinguished. Rationalizing intellectualists lay stress on deductive and dialectic arguments, making great use of abstract concepts and pure logic. Hegel, Bradley, Taylor and Royce are examples. Empiricist intellectualists are more scientific and think that the character of the world must be sought in our sensible experiences and found in hypotheses based exclusively thereon. Clifford, and Pearson are examples of this type. These insist that in our conclusions personal preferences should play no part, and that no argument from what ought-to-be to what is, is valid. Faith, being the means of contact between our whole nature and a kind of world conceived as well as adapted to that nature, is forbidden. All judgment must be suspended until purely intellectual evidence that such is the actual world has come in. James considers this the general rule of intellectualism.[55]

According to James, the position of intellectualism may be summarized as follows: First, intellectualism postulates that our paramount duty is to escape error. Second, it postulates that in every respect the universe is finished in advance of our dealings with it; that the knowledge of what it is, is best gained by a passively receptive mind. Finally, our beliefs and facts are mere externalities and cannot alter the universe as it is discovered.

This view does not satisfy James, even though he

does agree that these postulates may work well with the interpretation of some data. Such details exist in advance of our opinion; truth concerning them is often of no pressing importance, and by believing nothing we escape error while we wait. But even here we often cannot wait but must act.[57]

The very presence of evil in the temporal order is the condition of the perfection of the eternal order, says Royce.[58] The Absolute is the richer for every discord and for all the diversity which it embraces, says Bradley.[59] But James concludes that while Royce and Bradley endeavor to explain away evil and pain, these are the conditions of which we are conscious in our daily experience and we must consider what people experience as reality; for only by experiencing reality may we know what it is.[60]

The philosophical dilemma is viewed in its historical context by James. Historically we find the terms intellectualism and sensationalism used as synonyms of rationalism and empiricism. It seems to be a natural tendency for intellectualism to take an idealistic and optimistic direction. Empiricists, on the other hand, are frequently materialistic, and their optimism is apt to be decidedly conditioned. The two tendencies are categorized by James as follows:

| *The Tender-Minded* | *The Tough-Minded* |
|---|---|
| Rationalistic | Empiricist |
| (going by principles) | (going by facts) |
| Intellectualistic | Sensationalistic |
| Idealistic | Materialistic |
| Optimistic | Pessimistic |
| Religious | Irreligious |
| Free-Willist | Fatalistic |
| Monistic | Pluralistic |
| Dogmatic | Skeptical |

# FAITH AND REASON

Upon this observation James expresses his candid opinion:

> What you want is a philosophy that will not only exercise your powers of intellectual abstraction, but that will make some positive connection with this actual world of finite human lives. You want a system that will combine both things, the scientific loyalty to facts and the willingness to take account of them, the spirit of adaptation and accommodation, in short, but also the old confidence in human values and the resultant spontaneity whether of religious or romantic type. And this is then your dilemma. . . . You find empiricism with inhumanism and irreligion; or else you find a rationalistic philosophy that indeed may call itself religious, but keeps out of definite touch with concrete facts and joys and sorrows.[61]

With his own sin in mind and realizing the shortcomings of theories which lose contact with experience, James develops his own view. Accordingly, he agrees with Pascal and Bergson that ultimate principles may not be known by the rational method. It is apparent from this that he is justified in looking beyond discursive reason for the true knowledge he seeks. According to Chevalier, James began to formulate his own view in his essay on the *Will to Believe,* 1897, and in his *Conferences of California,* 1898. He remodels the pragmatic principle of Pierce and applies it specifically to religion. He illustrates it by the observations of his *Varieties of Religious Experience,* 1902. But he did not know it in all its ramifications, precision, meaning and metaphysical outreach until he treated his pragmatic principle in *Pragmatism,* 1907 and in the *Meaning of Truth,* 1909.[62]

In this chapter we see that Pascal arrives at his belief in the limitations of reason in a different manner from James and Bergson. His discovery is more dramatic; for even though we must take into account the scientific and philosophical influences behind his thought; it is the Second Conversion of Pascal which confirms his decision. He is acquainted with the rational method while, on the other hand, he witnesses to a higher type of knowledge which he experiences. The distinction between these two ways of knowing is clear in his mind, for he knows both by personal experience and, thus, he may contrast their differences. Contrast being more revealing than comparison, the contradictions of rationality are clear to us as he views them over against the higher synthesis, the Gospel.

Bergson and James likewise discover the limits of reason in their search for the real and the true. They realize that they must reject concepts as final and turn to experience for true knowledge beyond the reach of concepts. Their viewpoints may be trusted where they are proved useful or valuable, but Pascal's judgment is more accurate. Pascal knows the finitude of rationality in a two-fold manner: by what he discovers himself and by what God reveals. The illumination of Grace gives him certain knowledge. Dorothy Eastwood observes that "Pascal finds his center of gravity in heaven rather than on earth."[63] This is true of Pascal in general. It is likewise true of his judgment on the limits of discursive reason.

It can be seen from this that there are many points of agreement in the development and general trend of the philosophy of the three men whose writings are being studied here. In this chapter we have only been concerned with factors behind their conclusion that the rational method is finite. All three philosophers agree on this point, although they arrive at this conclusion differently. They offer suggestions for going

# FAITH AND REASON

beyond these limitations. This they do not by dismissing reason but by affirming its limits and ascribing its bounds, while they turn to experience, by intuition, for a deeper knowledge. They tell us, then, that the most important questions of our lives are not answered by the rational hypothesis, and that there must be another way of knowing. With this in mind, we turn to their discussion of supra-rational knowledge.

## CHAPTER II

## THE ATTAINMENT OF
## SUPRA-RATIONAL KNOWLEDGE

We have shown that Pascal, Bergson and James agree that ultimate reality is beyond the limits of rational knowledge. This fact leads to an examination of what they have to say concerning knowledge of ultimate reality. We have viewed their conclusions with regard to reason; now let us observe their contribution to faith. The use of the term supra-rational knowledge is to be interpreted as faith in this study. However, faith as used here has a broad meaning. It is not limited to religious faith. First, it includes taking a chance on the basis of possibilities. Second, it embraces knowledge immediately apprehended. Finally, faith includes religious belief in a general sense and also in its unique sense, i.e. general as used by James in his *The Will To Believe* and unique as used by Pascal who speaks of a saving knowledge through Jesus Christ.

There is agreement between Pascal, Bergson and James upon religious faith defined in its broad sense. Pascal is the only one who uses faith in the unique sense of saving knowledge. He speaks of illumination of the personality by Grace and insists that God inclines the heart to believe. Let us turn first, then, to the examination of Pascal's writings to see what he means by faith, and how he relates it to reason.

## FAITH AND REASON

### A. Pascal On The Primacy Of Faith

The clue to Pascal's *Apology* is his statement that *"le coeur a ses raisons que la raison ne connait point: on le sait en mille choses."*[1] When Pascal speaks of reason, *la superbe raison,* he means pure reason or discourse, the typical reasoning of the dogmatist.[2] This type of reason is assigned by Pascal an instrumental function. He does not seek to dismiss it but to ascribe its limits.

> It is necessary, says Pascal, to know how to doubt where necessary, affirm where necessary, submit where necessary, anyone who does not act thus does not understand the strength of reason. There are some who fail in relation to these three principles, either by affirming everything for lack of knowing where it is necessary to submit oneself; or by submitting oneself in everything for lack of knowing where it is necessary to judge. True Christianity consists in the submission and use of reason.[3]

Reason is slow to act and often fails for lack of necessary evidence or facts, while feeling is instant and always ready to act. Feeling and faith, according to Pascal, belong together, and concerning this he says: "It is the heart that feels God, and not reason. That is what faith is."[4]

Tollemache calls our attention to an excellent commentary of this view by Arnauld: "Contrition and love of God are acts of the will, and acts of the will are not thoughts, but motions, inclinations . . . and leanings of the heart towards its object."[5]

The heart as Pascal uses it has a Hebraic relation and is conceived as the center of the human personality.[6] According to the Biblical reference cited the heart includes thought, feeling and will and represents the whole personality in its inmost being. It integrates every energy of a man in the service of a cause to which he owes allegiance. Reason cannot command our complete loyalty, and thus ultimate things are known by the heart.

According to Chevalier:

> In Pascal's work, as in the language of the day, and in the scripture, the heart denotes the most secret part of our being . . . It is one of the instruments of knowledge and the origin of our intellectual operations. . . . Between the heart and reason, Pascal establishes a distinction akin to the Greeks between νοῦς and διανοια pure thought and discursive thought. . . . The heart, in Pascal's view, is essentially the direct apprehension of principles, including knowledge and feeling together.[7]

Pascal does not mean that faith is merely a matter of feeling. The principles to which the heart is attached are facts above us. The heart does not effect proofs, but grasps their significance and effects their synthesis. Reason is full of contradictions and in the end must surrender to a higher type of knowledge. Reason puts in a claim, but it is swayed in every direction.

> Those who judge a work by intuition are, in comparison to others like men who wear a watch. One says: "Two hours ago"; another says, "Only three-quarters of an hour ago." I glance at my watch and say to the former: "You are getting bored" and to the latter: "With you time gallops; for it is just an hour and a half," and I laugh at those who say that with me time drags, and that I count by fancy. They do not know that I count by my watch.[8]

This sums up what Pascal means by "the heart has reasons that reason does not know."[9] The nature of this knowledge is that which leads to salvation. Before Jesus Christ, according to Pascal, men did not know where they were and could only guess without knowledge and by chance. Faith differs from proof; it is implanted in the heart and is a gift of God. It is clear that Pascal speaks of revealed knowledge and of the Christian's God. This God is no Idea, First Cause, etc., but the God of Abraham, of Isaac and Jacob, the God

# FAITH AND REASON

Who reveals Himself in Christ. Accordingly, Pascal refers to the God, not of philosophers, but of believers and faith in this God is saving knowledge.[10] Here Pascal agrees with John in his Gospel, "And this is eternal life, that they know thee the only true God and Jesus Christ whom thou hast sent."[11]

The metaphysical proofs of God, says Pascal, are so involved that they are useless. They are unconvincing and grant no security. This is true of any knowledge of God apart from Jesus Christ and is the mere communion with God without a mediator. This is no true God, for as John has said, "grace and truth came through Jesus Christ."[12] Pascal says:

> . . . Christianity consists strictly in the mystery of the Redeemer, who, uniting in Himself two natures, divine and human, has delivered men from the corruption of sin in order to reconcile them to God through His divine Person.[13]

Jesus Christ is the center of everything and to know him is to understand all things. God cannot be known apart from the awareness of our misery and our misery cannot be known without the knowledge of God. Thus through our knowledge of God in Jesus Christ we know at once our misery and God, as well as our relief. God, the Father of Our Redeemer, is a God of love and consolation, Who fills the soul and heart of His purchased ones making them conscious of their misery and their hope, which is His gift of salvation.[14]

> The universe is for the sake of Jesus Christ. He is the fulfilment of prophecy; the Liberator who was predicted by the prophets of Israel. He came to suffer and die for us on earth in time. According to Scripture God is hidden. Ever since the corruption of nature He has left men to blindness from which there is no escape save through Jesus Christ and without Him no communication with God is possible . . . "no one knows the Father except the Son and anyone to whom He chooses to reveal Him."[15]

All religions have tried and failed, says Pascal. Let us accept the revelation of God in Christ. If we commune with God it is by Grace and if we are humbled it is by repentance. God wills to redeem us and open the way of salvation to those who seek Him. Other religions are false in that they advance reasoning as a means of attaining belief while, in fact, faith is God's gift.[16]

The Christian's God makes the soul feel that He is her rest, her joy and strength. In Jesus Christ all opposites are harmonized, for He is man's true God.[17] Without Him man must abide in misery. In Him lies all our virtue and felicity; without Him our lot is vice, misery, error, darkness and despair.[18] We cannot know ourselves except through Christ and without Him we know not the meaning of our life, or our death, or God. Without Scripture, which has Jesus Christ alone as its object, we know nothing, and see only the obscurity and confusion in the nature of God and nature itself.[19]

We should not be astonished to see simple people believe without reasoning, for God gives them love of Him and hatred of themselves by inclining their hearts to believe. One will never believe with a useful belief and real faith, if God does not incline his heart, but one will believe as soon as God inclines his heart.[20] Accordingly, instead of complaining that God is hidden we should thank Him for His revelation and that He has not disclosed Himself to the proud who are unworthy of His holiness.[21]

> Jesus Christ is Redeemer of all. . . . He made the offer, like one who has ransomed all willing to come to Him. If some die on the way, it is their misfortune; for His part, He offered them Redemption. . . . Jesus Christ, as Redeemer, is absolute master of all; and thus He is Redeemer of all, so far as in Him lies.[22]

# FAITH AND REASON

In his famous Wager Argument, Pascal applies the law of probability to the question of the existence of God, showing that so much is gained and so little lost by wagering that He does exist, so little gained and so much lost if He does not exist. Reason and self-interest combine to indicate choice of belief in His existence as the sensible one to make. The Wager Argument is designed to grip the whole man and move him from indifference to a decisive choice.

According to Pascal the existence of God is incomprehensible, but it is just as incomprehensible to believe that He does not exist.[23] Incomprehensibility is no criterion for truth or falsity. Reason is also incapable of judgment. Finite creatures cannot know of themselves what the infinite God is like, nor whether He exists. We are obligated, nevertheless, to choose between the existence or non-existence of God by weighing the merit of both decisions.

> You have two things to lose, truth and goodness, and two things to stake: your reason and your will, your knowledge and your beatitude; and your nature has two things to flee, error and misery. . . . You must necessarily choose. Let us weigh the gain and loss of choosing that God is. . . . If you win, you win everything; if you lose, you lose nothing. . . . There is here an infinity of infinitely happy life to win, one chance of winning against a finite number of chances of losing, and what you stake is finite. That removes all hesitation: wherever infinity is, where there is not an infinity of risks of losing against that of winning, there is no need to weigh matters, you must stake everything. . . . Our proposition has infinite force when a finite stake is to be risked in a game where there are equal chances of gain and loss and infinity is to be won.[24]

When his interlocutor seeks a more convincing statement, Pascal continues:

> . . . Your inability to believe, since reason leads you to do so comes from your passions. Labour then, not to convince yourself by increasing the number of proofs of God, but by lessening

your passions. You want to go to faith, and you ask the remedy of it: learn from those who have been bound like you, and who now wager all they have; they are people who know this way that you want to take, and who are cured. Begin the way they did: *that is by acting just as if they believed, taking holy water, having masses said, etc. Naturally, even that will make you believe* . . .[25]

Pascal uses great skill to make this argument convincing. He desires to remove all the obstacles which prevent the unbeliever from seeing clearly the eternal issues at stake in his choice for or against the God of Christians. He seeks to remove the indifference of intellectual pride. He desires to arouse in the unbeliever a deep concern for his destiny and insists that it is more reasonable to believe in God than to disbelieve in Him. Pascal says passions must be fought, for they are great obstructions to faith. No proofs can coerce conversion on a man, for he must be in the receptive mood.[26]

Chevalier has observed that before entering upon the proofs of the Christian religion, Pascal seeks to lead men to see that God conceals Himself from those who tempt Him. Men must take sides in this instance and they must do so voluntarily. "It is the setting of the will to work that is needed. We must make men decide to take the step, and for this purpose, in Pascal's mind, the argument of the wager will serve."[27]

Pascal concludes that it is not certain that religion tells us absolute truth; neither is it certain that religion does not. Nevertheless, it is reasonable to work for tomorrow, for according to the law of loss and gain, we work for the uncertain. By the rule of chances one should take the trouble to seek truth, for one is lost who dies without adoring the true cause. One should have far more fear of being mistaken and of discover-

# FAITH AND REASON

ing that Christianity is true, than of not being mistaken and of believing it to be true.[28]

> It is no use saying that our gain is uncertain and our risk certain, and that the infinite distance between *certainty* of what we stake and the *uncertainty* of what we gain, equals the finite good which is certainly staked against the uncertain infinite, for this is not the case. Every gambler risks a certainty to gain a finite uncertainty, and that without transgressing reason. There is not an infinite distance between the certain stake and the uncertain gain and certainty of loss. But the stake, according to the proportion of the chances of gain and loss. Hence it comes that where there are as many risks on the one side as on the other, the game is even; and then the certainty of stake is equal to the uncertainty of the gain; they are far from being infinitely separated. And so our argument is of infinite force when there is the finite to stake in a game in which the chances of gain and loss are equal, and the winnings are infinite. This is demonstrable and if men are capable of any truth, this is one.[29]

It is the opinion of the author that the Wager Argument is an integral part of Pascal's *Apology*. The issue involved is the basis of his faith and this argument is his way of making the issue of importance to others. This position concerning the Wager will be developed in the last chapter of this study.[30]

## B. Bergson on Intuition: Open and Dynamic Manifestations

In Bergson supra-rational knowledge or the knowledge of faith is found in his emphasis upon intuition as the only means of knowing reality in itself.

Let us examine Bergson's theory of knowledge. He states that instinct perfected is a faculty of using and even of constructing organized instruments.[31] Instinct is not the same thing as intelligence, but is not beyond the limits of mind. There is an interpenetration between intellect and instinct. Accordingly, his theory of knowledge is related to his theory of life.

The difference between intelligence (in the strictly scientific sense) and intuition is partly a difference of methods, and purpose. Intelligence is the faculty of manufacturing artificial objects, especially tools to make tools. Its concepts are regarded as fixed and definite, and we manipulate them as though they were tools. Intellect works with what is given and does not seek to apprehend the individuality of the real, but to "reconstitute" it with given, and stable elements.[32]

Intuition is defined as, "a kind of intellectual sympathy by which one places oneself within an object in order to coincide with what is unique in it."[33] As sympathy, intuition is associated with instinct: "By intuition," says Bergson, "I mean instinct that has become disinterested, self-conscious, capable of reflecting on its object and enlarging it indefinitely."[34]

Dorothy Eastwood has observed that Bergson attributes the sense of the real to the inner life. The search for the solution of existence is found in the inward rather than the external world. His conception of liberty, memory, intuition and life itself is inward. This affirms in outline Pascal's view, Eastwood points out.[35] Bergson is opposed to scientific dogmatism and insists that there are two ways of knowing a thing; from within and from without.[36] Personality must be regarded as the most positive reality known to our experience. Accordingly, Bergson's concept of personal duration is a complete reversal of the typically scientific attitude, which had regarded personal consciousness as an 'epiphenomenon' of matter. Eastwood says:

# FAITH AND REASON 45

> Reason can deal only with quantity; therefore, mathematics are its most perfect expression; the characteristic hypothesis of science is the conservation of energy. Even with reference to the material world this hypothesis is not absolute, and to the human personality it is wholly inapplicable; for there, in a far higher degree than in the stride of Achilles, time is indeniably a continuum, qualitative and incalculable so that reason has no grip of it.[37]

Bergson's thesis in *Two Sources of Morality and Religion*[38] can be best understood against the background of his *Creative Evolution*. Closed *morale* and static religion correspond to the inertia of mechanism and automatism, while open *morale* and dynamic religion represent the formal movement of the vital impetus. The former type is characteristic of the human species as a temporary stopping-place in the advancing movement, while the latter expresses the effort of life to lift mankind to a higher level. The greater part of religion is said to be static because Bergson believes it is among the forces making for stability in human societies, while mysticism is regarded as a dynamic force contributing to social mobility.[39]

Bergson believes that there is a way in which the vital forces of religion may be used in the furtherance of wider and more permanent ends. By intuition man can make contact with the vital impetus and allow it to work through him. By realizing his identity with this principle of life, he may realize its energies for a creative advance.[40] The essence of mysticism, Bergson insists, is not contemplation but action and its goal is not ecstasy; rather, it is an identification with the *élan vital*, and participation in its creative advance. He subordinates the intellectual to the intuitive element of experience. Mysticism is for him strongly volitional and its significance lies in action, in the type of life to which it leads.[41]

What Bergson calls a *new emotion*[42] is the source of great creations, for it incites the intelligence to take ventures and the will to persevere with them. Accordingly, it is that which stirs the soul and is an upheaval of the depths. It is supra-intellectual and is that which drives intelligence forward being productive of ideas. In this respect, creation signifies emotions, for this new emotion vivifies and vitalizes the intellectual elements with which it is destined to unite, all for a creative advance.[43]

> Antecedent to the new *morale* and also the new metaphysics, there is the emotion which develops as an impetus in the realm of the will, as an explicative representation in that of intelligence. Take for example, the emotion introduced by Christianity under the name of charity: if it wins over souls, a certain behaviour ensues and a certain doctrine is disseminated. But neither has its metaphysics enforced the moral practice nor the moral practice introduced a disposition to its metaphysics. Metaphysics and *morale* express the same thing, one in terms of intelligence, the other in terms of the will and the two expressions of the thing is there to be expressed.[44]

Our intelligence and our language deal in fact with things. The *morale* of the Gospels is that of the open soul. There is the act by which the soul opens, broadens and raises to a pure spirituality that *morale* which is materialized. This is the message of the Sermon on the Mount. The dynamic absorbs the static and the latter becomes a mere instance of the former.[45]

Bergson reminds us that between the open soul and the closed soul there is the soul in the process of opening; between the static and dynamic there is a *morale* in a transitional stage. The purely static *morale* is infra-intellectual, while the dynamic is supra-intellectual; the former is less than intelligence, while the latter is more than intelligence and between the two lies intel-

## FAITH AND REASON

ligence. The human soul normally settles down at the point of intelligence, but to go beyond intelligence is to reach intuition and the creation of the open soul.

> But there is only one road leading from action confined in a circle to action developing in the freedom of space, from repetition to creation, from the infra-intellectual to the supra-intellectual. Anyone halting between the two is in the zone of pure contemplation, and in any case, no longer holding to the one but without having yet reached the other, naturally practices that half-virtue detachment.[46]

Reason, Bergson states, is the distinguishing mark of man, but reason is not all; for it can only put forth reasons which are at liberty to counter other reasons.[47] Accordingly, the Bergsonian conception of open *morale* is based upon the mystic experience rather than upon reason.

> I mean mystic experience taken in its immediacy, apart from interpretation. True mystic experience is one in which the soul is open to the oncoming wave. That which the mystics allow to flow into them is a stream flowing down and seeking through them to reach their fellowman; the necessity to spread around them what they have received affects them like an onslaught of love.[48]

The philosopher searches in the social environment and finds in each principle only the morality he puts there. On the other hand, dynamic morality *(morale)* is impetus and creates nature which in turn creates social demand; its aspirations are supra-rational. Intelligence intervenes to seek the intellectual content by systematic analysis. It tries to reduce the motivation to a single fact, but the truth is that an idea which becomes obligatory is already active and made thus by its action and we only name the impetus which is already sweeping us forward.[49]

True mysticism is rare. It is the overt manifestation

of the drive of the *élan vital*. As a result of this mystic experience a mixed religion arises which implies a new direction given to the old. The ancient god who emanated from the myth-making function is merged into the God who effectively reveals Himself, who illuminates and warms privileged souls with His presence.[50]

The man who has the mystic experience, of which Bergson speaks, is not pride-ridden; rather, he is very humble upon feeling the Divine Presence; for he realizes his unworthy state and envisions the scope of his task of duty.[51] The true mystic feels it incumbent upon him to teach mankind, for he knows of the love of God for all men. He knows the divine love of God for his handiwork, which is also creative, being the source of all things. With the help of God, the mystic desires to help complete the creation of the human species and to make of humanity what it would have become were it not for the assistance of man himself. Accordingly, this love is the *élan vital*, communicated in its entirety to exceptional men who in turn would impart it to humanity at large. His anxiety to lift humanity up to God is predicated upon the realization that the true end of man may never be realized without the help of God.[52]

After studying many kinds of mystics, Bergson concludes that the Christian mystics bear an inner revelation.[53] Theology includes, according to Bergson, the *élan vital* in its formulations.[54] Christ shows us the divinity of all men and this is true whether he was man or not. In fact, says Bergson, the existence of Jesus has nothing to do with the fact of the Sermon on the Mount; nevertheless, the Gospels do have an author and the great mystics are imitators of what the Christ of the Gospels was completely.[55] Bergson reminds us that Christianity owes much to the Jewish prophets

# FAITH AND REASON

who were actively mystical and "capable of marching on to the conquest of the world."[56]

The mystic experience is a good criterion for establishing the existence of God, Bergson insists, for philosophy can discuss this problem in no other way. Accordingly, for an object to be known to exist it must be perceived; that is the object must be presented in actual or possible experience.

> ... You may construct the idea of an objective being as the geometrician does for a geometrical figure; but experience alone will decide whether it actually exists outside of the idea thus constructed. ... When most philosophers speak of God they are so remote in their conception from the God most men have in mind that if by some miracle ... God as thus defined should step down into the field of experience, none would recognize Him. Religion ... regards Him above all, as a Being who can hold communion with us.[57]

The deep-seated agreement of Christian mystics may be due to a common tradition or training but it is far more a sign of an identity of intuition which points to the actual existence of a Being with Whom they believe themselves to hold communion. Experience is the only source of knowledge. The mystic views love as the very essence of God and this love has an object or it is void of meaning; thus God loves us and needs us, just as we need Him. Bergson views creation as God's undertaking to create creators that He may have beings worthy of His love. "God is love," says Bergson, "and the object of love. Here is the whole contribution of mysticism."[58]

Bergson, as well as Pascal, considers faith or suprarational knowledge as accompanying communion with God, but they differ in their description of the manner of this communion. Bergson tells us that communion with God is direct by means of the mystic intuition; on the other hand, Pascal declares that communion with God is possible only through the Mediator, Jesus Christ. Accordingly, it is evident that Bergson does the best he can to describe faith, but at the same time being limited by his metaphysic and without theological support. On the other side of the account, Pascal begins with his "reasons of the heart," which resemble what Bergson calls intuition, but he has the additional knowledge of faith which personal knowledge of God through Christ affords.[50] Bergson's view is closer to that of James than to that of Pascal as we shall soon observe.

C. JAMES VIEWS FAITH AND THE RIGHT-TO-BELIEVE

We turn again to William James for a consideration of supra-rational knowledge. We must remember that James is both a psychologist and a philosopher. By faith, James means taking a chance on the basis of *possibility*. The word, faith, may be applied to venture in all phases of life and supra-rational knowledge is based upon experience; for reality is known by immediate apprehension.

James thinks of consciousness as a stream of flowing time, and he holds that empirical description of consciousness must begin with this stream. There is no distinction between feeling and thought; for feeling is immediately cognitive, i.e., it has an object which it knows. Feeling is a perception, conception, etc.: its knowledge *about* a thing is knowledge of its relations.[60] The stream of thought is continuous, for there are no psychical atoms. Accordingly, present thought is enriched by all the past experiences of the individual,

# FAITH AND REASON

and future thought will be further enriched by what it inherits from the present.[61]

As a result, *self* is a very complex motion built up from the experiences of "warmth," intimacy and felt continuity, which are handed down from thought to thought, becoming more abstract as they are thus made a matter of inheritance. The kind of experiences, which have this peculiar "warmth," are those primarily which center around interest and activity; that is around voluntary life. The notion of *self* is that of an intimate activity; that is, around the voluntary life. The *self* then is the notion of an intimate activity which has become very "warm" through emphasis and the element of activity, when carrying this "warmth" of personal identity is the feeling of *self*.[62] The will, James maintains, is conscious of a mental fiat which cannot be put in the effect-category; it is the ground of acquaintance with *self* in the normative case *I*, as opposed to what I know about *self*, in the objective sense, *Me*. On this basis James arrives at his principle that the present thought is a spiritual presence which is all that preceding impulses were, and it has a selective spontaneity of its own.[63]

The epistemology of James may be understood only by an acquaintance with pragmatism and its presuppositions. Perry gives the following definition:

> The pragmatist theory of knowledge . . . is an analysis and description of the concrete process of intellection or reflective thought. It is an account of mediate knowledge, or knowledge about — of that knowledge in which ideas of things (are entertained, believed, or verified).[64]

A pragmatist sees reality in terms of its process and circumstances, while the horizon of the intellectualist is bound by the intellect. The pragmatist vitalizes the intellect, while the intellectualist intellectualizes life. The real support of the pragmatic viewpoint lies in the insistence upon the validity of a non-intellectual type of knowledge which is more fundamental and more comprehensive than intellection; for intellectual knowledge is surrounded and corrected by intuitive or immediate knowledge. The only way, according to James, to apprehend reality is to dive into the flux itself, that is turn to sensation.[65]

James applies his method of radical empiricism to the study of religion. The psycho-physiological ensemble of which religious phenomena form a part is considered; then these are distinguished from concomitant and related phenomena, and a religious element *per se* is established. Religion is a personal affair; there are as many forms of religious experience as there are individuals. In justifying the rational value of religious experience, James attacks his problem from the pragmatic viewpoint and contends that the result of a religious life is sanctity. Religious experience is not by itself objective; for faith is a necessary condition of some of its effects, gives it an objective character and is the basis of all knowledge.[66] Accordingly, James insists that we should cherish our hopes rather than our fears by appealing as a psychologist to the facts of human consciousness to show the probability of the kind of spiritual world in which he believes.[67]

His thesis in *The Will to Believe* is that when we are presented with a forced option between two alternatives, both of which are genuinely alive but neither of them demonstrable, the course of wisdom is for us to choose tentatively on the basis of our hopes rather than

# FAITH AND REASON

our fears, and to act as if they were true; for we have the right to such beliefs as help us to live our lives.[68]

In his *Principles of Psychology*, James had formerly emphasized the intimate relation of attention to belief and physical action. "We need only in cold blood act," he says, "as if the thing in question were real, keep acting as if it were real, and it will infallibly end by growing into such a connection with our life that it will become real." And he continues, "those to whom 'God' and 'Duty' are mere names can make them much more than that if they make a little sacrifice to them every day."[69]

Let us now examine more carefully the manner James views faith and the right-to-believe. In *Varieties of Religious Experience*, James characterizes the religious life in the belief that there is an unseen order. Our good lies in our harmonious adjustment to this unseen realm; for "this belief and this adjustment are the religious attitude in the soul."[70] He contends that in the human consciousness is found a sense of reality, a feeling of objective presence, a perception of what we may call something there which is, "more deep and more general than any of the special and particular senses by which the current psychology supposes existent realities to be originally revealed."[71] For example, says James, Luther believed Christ to have done his work well, which is faith in a fact intellectually conceived. But this is only a part of Luther's faith, the intellectual part. The remainder of Luther's faith was intuitive, viz. the assurance, "that *I* this individual *I*, just as *I* stand, without one plea, am saved now and forever."[72]

According to James, it is safe to say that personal

religious experience has its root and center in mystical states of consciousness. Mystical states have a noetic quality; for even though they are similar to states of feeling, they seem to those who experience them to be also states of knowledge. They are illuminations and carry usually a sense of authority for an after-time.[73] Through the subconscious, James seeks to establish his position by insisting that there is more life in our total soul than we are at anytime aware of.[74]

> Let us propose as a hypothesis, that whatever it may be on its *farther* side, the *more* with which in religious experience we feel ourselves connected is on its *hither* side the subconscious continuation of our conscious life. . . . The Theologian's contention that the religious man is moved by an external power is vindicated, for it is one of the peculiarities of invasions from the subconscious region to take on objective appearances and to suggest to the subject an external control. In the religious life the control is felt as higher but since on our hypothesis it is primarily the higher faculties of our own hidden mind which are controlling, the sense of union with the power beyond us, is a sense of something, not merely apparently, but literally true.[75]

The conscious person, James contends, is continuous with a wider self through which saving experiences come. The further limits of our being plunged into another dimension of existence distinct from the sensible and understandable world and this other region is the world of our ideal impulses. We have a greater affinity with this invisible region than the visible; for we belong in a very intimate sense wherever our ideals belong. But this unseen region is more than ideal, for it produces effects in this world and by communion with this unseen region, our personality is enriched, we become new men and lead better lives. That which produces effects in another reality must be a reality itself, and, for this reason, one has no excuse for calling the unseen or mystical world unreal.

# FAITH AND REASON

> God is the natural appellation for us Christians . . . for the supreme reality, so I call this higher part of the universe by the name of God. We and God have business with each other; and in opening ourselves to His influence our deepest destiny is fulfilled. The universe takes a turn genuinely for the worse or for the better in proportion as each one of us fulfills or evades God's demands.[76]

The pragmatic way of taking religion is the deeper way, says James; for it gives to religion the characteristic of fact. He is willing by virtue of his over-beliefs to make a personal venture assuming that even though we may not know what the divine facts are, we should believe that they exist.[77] "In a word, the believer is continuous, to his own consciousness, at any rate, with a wider self from which saving experiences flow in."[78] Those who have such expression are unmoved by criticism for they know that they inhabit an invisible spiritual environment from which help comes. They know that the soul is mysteriously one with a larger soul whose instruments we are.[79] Accordingly, we are parts of God and not external creations. God is himself a part of the pluralistic universe; his functions are similar to ours.[80] This is for James the only reasonable conclusion to make concerning the nature of God. He cannot accept the traditional Christian concept of God, for it is completely out of harmony with his pragmatic and pluralistic notions.

We live in a multiuniverse, one in which we may decide what the future will be. There is nothing extant capable of preventing the *possible*, James declares. The absence of real grounds of interference may thus be said to make things *not possible* in the bare abstract sense. Most *possibles* are not bare, rather, they are concretely grounded. Pragmatically, this means that some of the conditions of production of the *possible* thing actually are here and when conditions become complete they are no longer *possible*, they are *actual*. When this notion is applied to the world it means that some of the conditions of the world's deliverance do actually exist.[81]

Midway between pessimism and optimism there is what James calls "meliorism," which treats progress as a *possibility* the more numerous the actual conditions become.[82] This is the inclination of pragmatism, which takes into consideration moments of discouragement and chance, but insists, nevertheless, that we must face tragedy and go beyond it believing that the *possible* may become the *actual*.[83]

> The true pragmatist is willing to live on a scheme of uncertified possibilities which he trusts; willing to pay with his own person, if need be for the realization of the ideals which he frames.[84]

Pragmatism, according to James, defends a willingness to live on *possibilities* that are not *certainties*, but sure anyway.[85] It may be called religious if religion be defined as pluralistic or melioristic in type, for it refrains from dogmatic answers. In fact, we do not know what type of religion is going to work best in the long run. Our over-beliefs and faith-ventures are needed to bring this evidence in.[86]

In his *The Will to Believe* James states that our nonintellectual nature directly influences our convictions and that human passions are stronger than technical rules. Our passional nature must decide an option between propositions, whenever it is a genuine option that cannot by its nature be decided on intellectual grounds; for to say, under such circumstances, "to not decide . . . is itself a passional decision . . . and is attended with the . . . risk of losing the truth."[87] Faith

## FAITH AND REASON

is hinged on the existence of truth, and, "we must know truth; and we must avoid error."[88] According to James, the empiricist does not give up the quest for truth, but desires truth intensely enough to seek to bring it into existence. His faith acts on the powers above him as a claim, and creates its own verification. For example, the question of having moral beliefs at all or not having them must be decided by the will, for if your heart does not *want* a world of moral reality, your head will never make you believe in one. In such case, faith will help create fact.[89]

The religious hypothesis, as James views it, is as follows: First, one should assume that the best things are the most eternal and are the ones which speak the final word. Second, we are better off if we believe the first affirmation to be true. Finally, we must accept religion as a momentous option. We gain even now by our beliefs and lose by our non-beliefs certain vital good.

> We cannot escape the issue by remaining skeptical and waiting for more light, because, although we do not avoid error in that way if religion be untrue, we lose the good if it be true, just as certainly as if we positively choose to disbelieve. . . . *Better loss of truth than chance of error*.[90]

Religious perspective is represented in the forming of personality. The universe is no longer a mere *It* to the believer, but a *Thou* and any relation that may be possible from person to person may also be possible here. Accordingly, James assures us that the trusting soul is rewarded for his religious perspective.[91]

James reminds us that the necessity to believe covers only live options, what may be or possibly could be true. Such belief is measured by action; that is by acting as if it were true. The whole defense of religious faith hinges on action and, thus, a decision is ever before us. We may hesitate if we will, but whether we choose or not we *act*, we take our lives into our own hands.[92] Our only way of doubting or refusing to believe, is to continue to act as if a thing were *not true*. This negative attitude is also a kind of action, for in the case of live options there is no neutral position. The human life is fraught with possibilities and no courageous act is performed except upon a possibility. Says James, "It is only by risking our person from one hour to the next that we live at all."[93] Accordingly, it is wise to believe what is in line with our needs, for in this manner they are fulfilled. It is often true that our faith in an uncertified result is the only thing that makes the result come true.

> I do not see why the very existence of an invisible world may not in part depend on the personal response which any one of us may make to the religious appeal. God Himself . . . may draw vital strength and increase of very being from our fidelity. For my part, I do not know what the sweat, blood and tragedy of this life means if they mean anything short of this. If this life be not a real fight, in which something is eternally gained for the universe by success, it is no better than a game of private theatricals from which one may with-draw at will. But it feels like a real fight, — as if there were something really wild in the universe which we; with all our idealities and faithfulness, are needed to redeem; and first of all to redeem our own hearts from atheisms and fears.[94]

According to James, a pluralistic universe with genuine possibilities squares with the belief in Providence; that is a Providence which offers *possibilities* as well as *actualities* in the universe. This means that *chances* exist uncontrolled by God and yet the end may be just as Providence intends for it to be. God may have thought out the universe prior to its creation, or rather suppose him to be thinking out the universe before he actually creates it. He knows the various points and

# FAITH AND REASON

possibilities, but leaves them open. But whatever may turn up as actual he knows what to do next to direct the universe to its proper end, the end of Providential design.[95]

In summary let us repeat that James insists that the character of the world's results may depend upon our acts and that our acts may depend on our faith, — our not resisting our faith-tendencies which go beyond rational evidence. He suggests the following as a faith ladder: We should believe, (1) that there is nothing absurd in a certain view of the world being true, nothing self-contradictory; (2) that it *might* have been true under certain conditions; (3) that it may be true, even now; (4) that it is fit to be true; (5) that it *ought* to be true; (6) that it *must* be true; and (7) that it *shall* be true, at any rate for *me*.[96] Accordingly, James considers faith as an inalienable birthright of our minds, and that it must go with the search for the most probable. We must have faith in spite of our awareness of risks as possibilities. Dilemmas come often in life, options may often be decisive, but we must take sides and go in for the most probable alternative as if the other did not exist and be willing to suffer what ever consequences may follow.[97]

> We must *trust* and do our *best* in spite of the *ifs*. If we do our best, the world will be perfected. We can *create* the conclusions to the fact in mind. We can and may, as it were, venture by trust and only so can the making of a perfect world of the pluralistic pattern ever take place. Only through our precursive trust in it can it come into being.[98]

In this chapter we have examined the theories of Pascal, Bergson and James concerning supra-rational knowledge or the knowledge of faith. All have turned to the inner life for their answer as to what faith is.

They affirm intuition or the "reasons of the heart" as basic and as a corollary to their basic presupposition, mystic experience is postulated. Pascal and James present their wager. We have not looked at their views critically, for that will be our task in the next chapter. We turn now to a critique of the previous discussion with the problem of faith and reason before us.

## CHAPTER III

## CONTRIBUTIONS TO THE PROBLEM OF FAITH AND REASON
## A CRITIQUE – CONCLUSION

### A. PASCAL AS CRITERION OF JUDGMENT

In Chapter I we were concerned with the discovery of the limitations of rational knowledge by Pascal, Bergson and James. We discussed how this discovery was made and hinted at their proposal to go beyond the rational method. In Chapter II we examined their definitions of supra-rational knowledge or faith. Our aim in this chapter is to criticize all that has gone before and to see what contribution each philosopher makes to our problem of faith and reason. At the close of this chapter we shall attempt to draw the resulting conclusions.

Pascal expresses in his *Pensées* an immediate knowledge of faith *par excellence*. We shall consider him as the criterion of judgment in this critique. He *lives* his faith, while Bergson and James *study* or *observe* those who experience faith. Even Bergson's *divine sympathy* is no substitute for a personal experience of faith on the order of Pascal's Second Conversion. Pascal confesses a divine illumination by Grace. He is true to the Augustinian doctrine of divine illumination of the human mind. Accordingly, he realizes that there are things man can never know unless God reveals them. Pascal appears as one who is "filled with the knowledge of His will in all wisdom and spiritual understanding."[1] He knows what may never be known by the approach of Bergson and James. He speaks with authority of a God felt in the heart. To know God, by the "reasons of the heart," is Pascal's definition of faith.

We intend to substantiate the thesis that even though James and Bergson have only a partial knowledge of what Pascal knows as a surety, they do have much in common, and that their agreement is basic. They all affirm intuition as primary in the search for reality. They also agree that the mystic experience is valid.

These brilliant thinkers make use of the most exact methods of science as a means of arriving at their conclusions concerning the limits of rational knowledge. With this background they postulate their suprarational hypotheses. Their former view stopped short of their desired destination, viz. reality at its source. This is the reason for their latter view. One must always be cautious of accepting a position which is critical of intelligence acquired by rational means. Such view could be less than discursive reason as well as more. However, Pascal, Bergson and James withstand the charge of irrationality. Pascal came by way of mathematics (especially geometry), science (physics) and a critical examination of philosophy ancient and contemporary to his affirmation of faith.[2] Bergson was acquainted with mathematics, biology, psychology, physiology and psychiatry. All these sciences contribute to his metaphysics.[3] James was efficient in anatomy, physiology, psychology, psychiatry and philosophy.[4] Accordingly, it is evident that they appreciate the rational method. It is by virtue of their thorough acquaintance with the rational method that they know its limitations. They find in it the incentive to develop their supra-rational theories.

They agree that the nature of supra-rational knowledge is immediate apprehension of truth and reality. They turn to the inner life for ultimate decisions. The things-in-themselves which are unknown, according to the rational method, are said to be known by intuition. This is their fundamental affinity. With this in mind we turn now to an examination of the "reasons of the heart."

### B. "The Reasons of the Heart" In Pascal, James and Bergson

Tillich suggests that Pascal uses the word "reasons" in a double sense when he speaks of the "reasons of the heart which reason cannot comprehend." The "reasons of the heart," Tillich calls the structures of aesthetic and communal experience (beauty and love); the reason, "which cannot comprehend them," is technical reason.[5] This is, I think, an accurate summary of Pascal's distinction between rational and supra-rational knowledge.

Cousin criticizes Pascal, asserting that the latter misuses the French in this passage. Cousin makes the most of the confusion of "reason" and "reasoning" — *"la raison"* and *"le raisonnement."* The expression *"le coeur"* is also challenged by Cousin. Pascal uses this term to designate the higher faculty of intuition as we have already observed.[6] The justification of this passage is found in the context of Pascal's thought; for there the meaning is clear. This is the presupposition behind Pascal's *Pensées*.

This affirmation of the "reasons of the heart" as primary is basic in the writings of Bergson and James also. The question may be raised, is it safe to accept a view which mistrusts rationality? One should make the further inquiry, may we rely upon the "heart" to differentiate between *infra* and *supra*-rational knowledge?

M. Cousin calls Pascal a "universal skeptic," one who embraced religion by exercising a blind faith in a sort of despair.[7] Who is right Pascal or Cousin? Keeping in mind the basic criticism of Cousin we may proceed in defense of Pascal. First, Pascal recognizes the value of rational evidence. He only holds that all things may not be arrived at by demonstration. He vindicates the principles of intuition presupposed in every exercise of reasoning. Second, even though Pascal points out the insufficiency of man he also seeks to lead him to a reconciliation of all contradictions in Jesus Christ.[8]

Clark has observed:

> Pascal was surely right when he held that men never had discovered the true nature of God without the aid of a supernatural revelation; and here he had the authority of St. Paul: "the world by wisdom knew not God" (I Cor. i.21); and of Christ: "No man knoweth the Son save the Father; neither doth any know the Father save the Son, and he to whomever the Son willeth to reveal Him." (Matt. xi.27).[9]

Perry holds that James and Bergson misunderstand the method of the intellectualists. He states that they fail to make clear whether a concept is to be understood by its function or content.[10] Perry's criticism is misdirected. Both James and Bergson give to intellect a distinct functional role.

According to Perry they confuse the relations of

# FAITH AND REASON

symbols and the relations symbolized.[11] The fact is, however, that they assign to the intellect and to science the role of analysis and symbolism. They make it clear that they protest the autonomy of the rational method and that things-in-themselves must be apprehended immediately rather than discursively.

Perry observes a distinction between James and Bergson concerning their critical view of intellectualism. He considers Bergson as a representative of an idealistic version of intuition while James represents a realistic version. Bergson states that intellect acts on matter from without. Conceiving is the process of creating concepts. A concept is a result of the activity of intellect.[12] On the other hand, James describes the intellect as selective. It discovers concepts which belong to reality.[13]

Accordingly, where James agrees with Bergson, Perry states that he fails to understand him. Otherwise James could not use Bergson to substantiate his own views. This is true especially where the former stresses certain dynamic and temporal properties as inconceivable. If to conceive is not to alter, but only to distinguish; then to mention a property with a view to show its inconceivability is to conceive it.[14] This difference between James and Bergson is obvious. However, what Perry has observed does not alter the affinity of James and Bergson on the limitations of rational knowledge. It is just as true that they unite in affirming the "reasons of the heart" as a means of knowing beyond rational concepts. Here Pascal, Bergson and James hold a single, basic presupposition.

Perry accepts James' view but continues to challenge Bergson. Bergson, he insists, considers concepts as *post mortem* leading to the negation of the essence of reality. Reality is not known by the connection of concept upon concept. There are no real connections according to intellectualism; for to distinguish according to conceptual logic is to be incapable of connection.[15] Perry disregards the fact that James has said the same thing in his 'flux of consciousness.' The defense of Bergson is given by James.[16] James thinks that Bergson does assign to concepts the role of disclosing to what quarter we may turn to find reality. "Bergson," says James, "is right in turning us away from conception to perception." The combination of old and new concepts is a theoretical achievement.[17] Concepts may tell us about visible objects but they cannot shed light on their interior. Bergson is correct to insist that the whole life of activity and change escape conceptual treatment.[18] This is a clear commentary of Bergson's own statement that there are two ways of knowing a thing. The first implies that we move around an object; the second that we enter into it. The former is the method of intellect, the latter is that of intuition.[19] Pascal agrees that the intellect cannot give us the knowledge of space, movement, time or number. The heart must feel these first principles just as it feels God.

> We know truth, not only by reason, but also by the heart; it is by this latter kind of knowledge that first principles are known and it is in vain that reason tries to understand them.[20]

Pascal adds:

"It is the heart that feels God, not reason. That is what faith is: God felt by the heart, not by reason."[21]

From this we may conclude that they accept as a starting-point what Pascal calls "reasons of the heart." Discursive reason is considered important by them, but their attention is given to developing a metaphysic

FAITH AND REASON 67

to go beyond concepts and make contact with the inwardness of reality. Their contribution to the problem of faith and reason is best understood in this context. The mystic experience is the logical outcome of their insistence upon the primacy of intuition. This fact becomes obvious when their principle of supra-rationality is applied to faith defined as religious. We turn now to an examination of the mystic experience as they view it.

### C. THE MYSTIC EXPERIENCE IN PASCAL, BERGSON AND JAMES

It is the opinion of the author that Pascal, Bergson and James contribute to the validity of the mystic experience. Pascal contributes more than the others. Dorthy Eastwood has well said:

> Eternity conceived as unapproachable by the addition of time to time, but an ever present now, supra-personal in essence, transcending duration as duration transcends space if it is to be touched at all, to be touched in an instant it must be on the order of the illumination of St. Augustine standing by the window of Ostia.[22]

Pascal's mystic experience resembles that of Augustine. Pascal bears personal testimony to the mystic experience as the way which leads to the ultimate solution of the human paradox. What Bergson and James know about other mystics Pascal knows within himself. Eastwood continues:

> To Pascal the night of the *Memorial* had brought *certitude* and *joie*, just as for the author of the Gospel of John truth makes men free. The demand *to know* arising from the success and limits of the scientific method, the upsurge of the demand *to be* characteristic of the "revival of energy" — stir to a new vigour the mystic aspiration, ever latent, in the conditions of human

life, towards a higher order or synthesis where contraries should be reconciled. And so it is by its relation to a fundamental antinomy in French thought and to a twofold impulse expressed in Bergson's philosophy of the real and Barres maxim "to be more possible," that Pascal appears as a climax and symbol of various tendencies which have borne him to his recent triumph.[23]

Bergson's idea of time as duration resembles Pascal's *ordre de la charité*. This is clearly seen in his treatment of mysticism. Bergson identifies dynamic religion with mysticism. In mysticism God acts through the soul and in the soul for creative advance. The soul envisions great things to be done in the Divine Presence and at the same time the zeal to seek their realization. He describes the Christian mystics as the greatest. Their God is creative love. This love moves the mystic to be useful to the purpose of God.[24] What he calls the supra-intellectual emotion is the mystic experience. Bergson admits going beyond the conclusions of *Creative Evolution*. In the former work he desired to keep close to facts, but now he is in the field of possibilities.[25] Philosophic certainty calls for intuition as well as for reason. If intuition, backed up by science, is to be extended, such extension can be made only by mystical intuition. It is significant that the mystic experience defined by Bergson culminates in a love which is active and creative.

According to Dorothy Eastwood, Bergson in developing his theory of three orders *(les corps, les esprits, la charité)* is close to Pascal. Bergson's insistence upon the transition from personal duration through reason to the extensity of matter resembles the philosophy of Pascal where reality is determined by its inwardness, the order of love being all inclusive. "In this way Pascal was felt to triumph by the triumph of personality in the Bergsonian doctrine."[26]

Berdyaev observes that true mysticism is supra-rational. It transcends symbols and turns to realities.²⁷ This is the spirit behind the mysticism of Bergson's thought. His mysticism is designed to lead to a life valued beyond the reach of reason. On the other hand he denounces a mysticism of pure contemplation. He leaves room for the autonomy of the personality and especially the will. He offers us a love which takes action in a creative advance and unites the theory of a union with God and that of practice. Self-knowledge and direction of life result from the experience of the Divine Presence. We are reminded of Pascal who states that the soul finds her strength and peace in God and that love of God is the sole desire of the Christian man.²⁸

Maritain observes that Bergson has made no worthwhile contribution to Christian doctrine, but from the viewpoint of intentions he is headed aright. He considers Bergson as making a mistake in his association of the *Two Sources* with *Creative Evolution*. By so doing, Maritain believes that Bergson reduces the spiritual to the biological context of the former work:

> I mean a biological itself made so transcendent that it is conceived as the creative source of all worlds, but which ever remains biological, in so far as the world relates to those levels of life, above all characterized by the organic and the physic, on which life manifests itself in the animation of matter, and on which consequently immanent activity is bound up with conditions of transitive action and of productivity. Of course it is true enough that outside the world of grace and of super-natural life man's spirituality never transcends the biological except in a more or less imperfect fashion.²⁹

Bergson has the wrong metaphysics to contribute to Christian doctrine. He rules out metaphysical reasoning. Bergson's *élan vital* does not square with Christian

Doctrine. The question of knowing this principle as the cause of all is secondary to Bergson, while to the Christian mystics it is primary to know the One to Whom they cling by faith. For the great mystics of Christendom to know God is life eternal.[30] This experience is, at once, love and supreme knowledge. Accordingly, Maritain states that Bergson's intentions are good but he has proven that a philosophy, in so far as it ignores the mystery of Grace and the Cross cannot attain the true nature of the mystical life. The Christian mystics do not turn to the *élan vital*, but to the depths of a Supreme Personality for communion. Bergson sees the divinity of all men and ascribes little value to the existence of Christ. There is no need for Christ as Mediator in his scheme. He is to be considered as a Supreme Example. At this point Bergson abandons the cardinal presupposition of Christian mysticism.[31] We may ask: Does Bergson understand the Christian mystics? Is he too anxious to view them in the light of his own metaphysics to understand them? Would it not be more profitable for us to go to the Christian mystics and study them directly?

Maritain is right to suggest that we turn to the Christian mystics themselves to answer our questions. The mystic experience of Pascal is a case in point. What he bears witness to is revealed knowledge. His communion with God is through Jesus Christ who is the center of all and all things to all people.[32] One sees in Bergson's *Two Sources* good intentions and one wishes that he had followed his spirit rather than his metaphysics. He needs theological support for his intentions which his thought-structure does not provide. He speaks of a great Christian virtue (love), but he is unable to make clear its definition.[33] His relation to the mysti-

# FAITH AND REASON 71

cism of Pascal is found in his intention, viz. his desire to commune with the essence of things. He falls short of Pascal who communes with God through Jesus Christ. God inclines Pascal's heart to believe and his contact with the Supreme Personality is by the illumination of Grace. Bergson's contribution lies in his uniting the unconscious and the mysterious in a process of mystic intuition. He considers the deeper self the true self.[34] Here we are on the threshold of the thought of James.

James supports both Pascal and Bergson in his psychological treatment of mysticism. He extricates the mysticism of Pascal from morbidity and fanaticism and justifies it in the sight of many who doubted its validity.

Dorothy Eastwood says:

> When the conscious ego is presented, not as an impervious entity, but as both subject to influences reaching it directly on its level from without, independently of material mediation, and as, moreover, certainly conscious by which it is liable at any time to be invaded, there may be felt to be nothing intrinsically unscientific or even improbable about the Christian doctrine of Grace.[35]

James insists that religion is a matter of feeling. The subliminal self is the true self. The subconscious mind is more potent than the conscious and less under the immediate domination of the material world. The mystic does not deny the value of reason but desires to penetrate deeper into the meaning of life than reason can direct him. He takes into account a larger world of meanings. To support this view, James presents his own "over-beliefs" as a hypothesis strictly relative to the data acquired. His pluralistic conception causes him to reject any mystic intuition presupposing union with the Infinite. He affirms the efficacy of prayer, and asserts that through the subconscious mind saving influences may enter the personal consciousness from some larger ego outside it.[36]

Dorothy Eastwood observes that James turns the discovery of the unconscious and its scientific principle into partial vindication of the mystic experience. His representation of reality under the aspect of consciousness rather than space, tends to enforce the conception of the orders in the writings of Pascal and Bergson. It gives to their basic thought the semblance of substantial, almost scientific actuality.[37]

James was not a mystic himself. He said to Pratt, who inquired if he were a mystic, "I believe in God, not because I have experienced his presence, but because I need it so that it must be true."[38] His personal faith and religious philosophy are reflected in a letter he wrote J. H. Leuba. In this letter James says:

> If mystical states with all their differences have a common nucleus, then this nucleus should be reckoned a co-ordinate factor with reason in the building up of religious belief. The intellect is interpretative and critical of its own interpretation, but there must be a thesis to interpret, and that thesis seems to me to be to a non-rational sense of a higher power. . . . It is evident that our data are complex . . . and that sifting is necessary. . . . The truth is what will survive the sifting by successive generations.
> 
> I find it preposterous to suppose that if there be a feeling of unseen reality shared by large numbers of best men in their best moments, responded to by other men in their "deep moments"; good to live by and strength giving, . . . to suppose that the goodness of that feeling for living purposes should be held to carry no objective significance and especially preposterous if it combines harmoniously with our otherwise grounded philosophy of objective truth.
> 
> My personal position is simple. I have no living sense of commerce with God. I envy those who have, for I know that the addition of such a sense would help me greatly. The Divine, for my active life, is limited to impersonal and abstract concepts which, as ideals, interest and determine me, but do so but faintly

in comparison with what a feeling of God might effect if I had one. This, to be sure, is largely a matter of intensity, but a shade of intensity may make one's whole center of moral energy shift.

Now although I am so devoid of *Gottesbewusstsein* in the directer and stronger sense, yet there is something in me which makes response when I hear utterances from that quarter made by others. I recognize the deeper voice. Something tells me thither is the truth. And I am sure it is not old theistic prejudices of infancy. Those in my case were Christian, but I have grown so out of Christianity that entanglement therewith on the part of a mystical utterance has to be abstracted from and overcome before I can listen. Call this if you like my mystical *germ*. It is a very common germ. It creates the rank and file of believers.

Dogmatic atheism or naturalism is a consistent position. Without any mystical germ at all in us, I believe that is where we would all be today. But the mystical germ points elsewhere.[39]

Accordingly, James is an observer of mystic experience. He accepts no special group of mystics as Bergson does for his standard, for this does not square with his metaphysics. However, he does seek to turn the discovery of the unconscious and the scientific principle of empiricism to a partial vindication of the mystic experience. He considers mysticism a type of supra-rational knowledge and insists that our rational consciousness is not the only form of knowledge. Using Pascal as our standard of judgment, the view of James receives a low rating. Pascal considers Christianity as the only true religion and communion with God through Jesus Christ as the only real mystic experience.[40] The view of James will not withstand this criterion. However, it is safe to maintain that there is a basic agreement in their interpretation of the faculty and validity of mystic experience.

In his view of mysticism James contributes to the validity of religious experience in general and the mystic experience in particular. His mysticism is no pure contemplation or union with an Absolute, rather, it inspires and enriches the mystic who will work to make a better world. He offers the mystic experience as a state of knowledge. His presupposition is related to Pascal's "reasons of the heart." However, James observes while Pascal experiences the mystic state. Pascal's treatment of mysticism has authority which that of James or Bergson have not; for they know as a *probability* what Pascal knows as a *certainty*. This is a clue to the difference between the wager of Pascal and that of James.

## D. The Wager Argument of Pascal and James

The question has often been raised, does the wager argument belong in the *Apology* of Pascal? Is it of great importance? If so upon what is this importance based? Strowski limits the significance of this argument by placing it at the beginning of his edition. He rejects it as a serious apologetic method calling it "an ingenious but cold and mechanical combination of abstract algebra and crude empiricism." It is useless as he sees it, for

> to believe is not to act as if God existed; it is to say God exists. The thing is not to decide if religion is advantageous, it is to find out if it is true. . . .[41]

According to Strowski, Pascal's wager will not produce an ounce of faith.

Renouvier, Dorothy Eastwood observes, finds the wager argument implicit in the doctrines of Locke, Bayle, Rousseau, Kant and James.[42] It sets forth a general principle — the inevitable position when the claim to complete deduction has been abandoned. Our

# FAITH AND REASON

future may depend on what we believe since belief is linked with conduct and thus the dilemma set forth by Pascal is actual.

In *The Will to Believe,* James states that Pascal tries to force us into Christianity by reasoning as if our concern with truth resembled our concern with stakes in a game of chance.[43] He dwells upon what Pascal says about masses and holy water. He insists that Pascal uses the gambling table as his last desperate snatch at a weapon against the hardened unbelievers. Nevertheless, James believes Pascal's personal faith to have a greater depth than that reflected in the argument.

I consider James' observation as false. He is judging Pascal's wager by his own pragmatism. James distinguishes between dead and live options.[44] and concludes that for Pascal's wager to be true it must be preceded by a pre-existing tendency to believe. For example masses would be considered a dead option for a good Protestant. We know that Pascal was loyal to the Church, from his writings. On the other hand, *The Provincial Letters* remind us that his personal convictions were primary; that he was not bound to the Church and that he condemned evils wherever found. The statement concerning masses and holy water is used by Pascal as an illustration because of its familiarity and his argument does not rise or fall with this illustration. Both Renouvier and James have shifted the point of the wager of Pascal. They lift the wager from its context and use it to support their pragmatic theses. They are right to insist that there is an imperative factor in moral decisions, but if this view is overemphasized the fundamental importance of the wager of Pascal is lost in its application.

Renouvier challenges Pascal's basic statement, viz. that God is or He is not. Renouvier contends that this is not the issue at all: moral interest and value which the intellect cannot decide are the objects of decision. Pascal, on the other hand, says exactly what he means; for to him, all depends upon the existence of God and that includes moral decisions of which his critics speak. Dorothy Eastwood has observed correctly that Pascal improves upon the view of his modern critics, by emphasizing the part played by voluntary intention in producing faith, and by regarding the will and physical acts as powerless in themselves to constitute faith. They simply prepare the way for faith. "In the wager," says Eastwood, "Pascal has set a precedent as the philosopher and psychologist of belief."[45]

When Pascal seeks to convince others through his wager argument he is not limited as are the moral pragmatists to 'live options.' If God the Father of Jesus Christ exists, He offers eternal life to all who believe in Him; thus, to know God, according to Pascal, is eternal gain; to not know Him is eternal loss. The issue is based upon a certainty in Pascal's own experience and, for this reason, tradition cannot be considered the final word of Pascal's faith or as the foundation of his wager. He uses the wager to reach those who may never be convinced otherwise; for he desires to be 'all things to all people that some might be saved.' His objective is to humble the proud and shock the indifferent to a concern for their eternal destiny. Accordingly, as we observe the wager we should never forget that Pascal believes strongly, "Whosoever would draw near to God must believe that he exists and that he rewards those who seek him."[46]

Cailliet substantiates this position by saying:

> The nature of the wager of Pascal has been terribly misjudged by making it a variation on the theme will-to-believe which the peripheral theory of James . . . was to elucidate. The fact is the argument of wager, according to a method familiar to Pascal, catches the free thinker at his own gamble and addresses him in the only language he understands, viz. that of human reason.
>
> Certainly, the reasoning of Pascal can convince the mind without securing action . . . But Pascal has well-realized this, and he is, in this sense a precursor of James . . . for he knows that action greatly overlaps the syllogisms of the intellect . . . and that one cannot dwell on this sufficiently since God exists, and since the searcher would not look for Him had he not already been found by him, each step in the new way will give rise to a revelation which will hence forth make his walk firmer and his path easier.[47]

The wager is an integral part of the *Apology* of Pascal, for it points up the necessity for decision as to whether God exists. The argument makes an appeal to the whole man and to all types of men. It is evident that if we view this argument in its context, with the understanding of its author, it is a worthwhile demonstration and one which removes obstructions from the way of faith.

We have seen that James uses the wager of Pascal to illustrate the way in which our desires may influence our beliefs. Pascal's wager is considered valid, by James, when the option is genuine. By the will-to-believe James does not mean what his critics contend, viz. that a man may believe anything he wishes and make it the truth. He means literally the right-to-believe as he states in his *Some Problems of Philosophy*.[48] James is striving to show that in certain cases the unaided intellect fails us, since the means for a purely intellectual decision are simply unavailable. He insists that even the intellectualist critics of his theory make passional decisions and exercise their will-to-believe in their choice of a philosophical standpoint.[49]

The question may be raised, how does one know what to choose when there are alternatives before him? James contends that the more creative alternative is the truer and is the realizer of greater possibilities. Accordingly, truth is distinguished from mere correctness by the criterion of utility. There may arise situations in which a decision is to be made when no absolute truth is available and in such a case truth may be created by the act. Our experience is one in which problems, crises and decisions are real. Truth is a process being made by our actions and is the success of our decisions and activities.

If we accept the view of James, the past presents a crucial problem. How can we verify a truth about an event in history? He distinguishes between the giveness of a fact and the truth of the belief about a fact. He states to convert a fact "Caesar is dead" into a proposition "that Caesar is dead" is to make room for all sorts of evasions. Having done so intellectualists are prone to confuse their belief that Caesar is dead with the fact and as a result make out a case for the absolute nature of their belief.[50] Past events, according to James, are past facts, but truth should be concerned with things which are verifiable, and, for this reason, looks ahead. James has no special concern for the past and loses little time arguing about it. In this particular his will-to-believe is related to faith, for faith looks ahead and its object is the unknown and unseen.

When James asserts that belief may be true let us therefore affirm it, isn't he really making a theoretic judgment? James meets this challenge by asserting that life is more than logic; that situations of decision arise for which theoretic knowledge is inadequate and incomplete and in such a case passional decisions are the only ones possible.

But is there any such thing as a forced option if the way is wide open? Is not doubt a possibility? According to James, doubt is the alternative to a forced option; thus the opposite of belief is not unbelief, but doubt. Accordingly, the question of faith is not a matter of faith or atheism, but of faith and skepticism and the choice is forced, we must decide.

James is protesting against the notion that the truth is established already, by contending that we make the truth along with our faith and effort. He offers us a message for the difficult circumstances of life, by urging us to be courageous. He brings together in *The Will To Believe* his reflections on the practical function of consciousness, and the interdependence of thinking, willing, and feeling processes of the human personality. He points out the kinship of belief and volition. He emphasizes the need of risk, of taking a chance and the verification of truth as a future possibility. His pragmatic theory is very much pronounced in his wager.

The will-to-believe and faith are related, says James. We are to trust in spite of evils and mystery and we must risk our lives and take chances for the good and the true. Some privileged souls have mystical experiences, which enable them to commune with unseen powers in a unique way. We all have a subliminal self, according to James, which makes it possible to realize the impact of the spiritual reality upon our lives and these powers are with us in our struggle for a better self and a better world. Accordingly, we all have the right-to-believe. This makes life worth living; for without faith life is nonsense.

In the wager of James we are urged to believe in *possibilities*. This is better than no faith at all; for he makes faith the basis of our entire life. Like Pascal, he bids us search our hearts for reasons which are beyond rationality and admonishes us to stake everything upon our faith. James seeks to verify faith by the support of the psychological principle of the subliminal self and his pragmatic theory. He has at least partial success in establishing the reasonableness of believing where we cannot prove. However, when we compare James with Pascal concerning the argument of wager, we discover that Pascal's insight of faith is more profound. While James in his notion of passional decision approximates what Pascal calls "reasons of the heart," James hinges his wager upon his pragmatic theory; while Pascal bases his entire argument upon the existence of God. Pascal asserts that knowledge and moral principles have significance only if God exists. Our heart feels Him, according to Pascal, and this is possible because God inclines the heart to believe in Him. As Brunner has said: "There is but one word strong enough to conquer despair and that is faith. Either we despair or we believe."[51] This is the theme of Pascal's *Pensées* including his wager.

### E. Conclusion

We are aware of the contribution made to the problem of faith and reason by the authors whose writings we have here examined. However, we are only partially satisfied with what Bergson and James offer, but

## FAITH AND REASON

we feel that what they seek Pascal has found. Joy, peace, certainty are expressed in his affirmation of faith and this is the kind of faith we need. He communes with God to receive a saving knowledge which comes through revealed truth and by the illumination of Grace.

James calls our attention to the flux of consciousness and the subliminal self for knowledge of our true self, reality and truth. He defines for us a faith that takes chances on possibilities. He emphasizes our right-to-believe and admonishes us to realize that there are many forced options; the faith of religion being one. This contribution is valuable so far as it goes; but it does not go far enough. James is limited by his method. For this reason, he limits God and places too much trust in what man *can* do. He is unable to decide upon any particular faith, for all is unfinished, and for this reason we must trust the future to make known which religious faith is best. We may observe from this, that there can be no certainty derived from the view of James; there is only probable belief based on possibility. However, his faith does take us beyond the rational and gives us courage to risk our lives for the good and the true; for inasmuch as we must take chances he urges us to do so for truth.

When we turn to Bergson, we find his answer to the problem of faith and reason in his mystic intuition. He speaks of a love that takes action. He contributes to the notion of faith, but we are immediately aware of shortcomings in his scheme of thought. His epistemology does not harmonize with Christian presuppositions. In Bergson, the *élan vital* is central, while in Christian thought (Pascal), the revelation of God in Christ is central. Bergson does mention some ethical and theological principles maintained by the Christian mystics, i.e. a God who reveals Himself, the Christian emotion of love, Christ as an example for mystics, and the Sermon on the Mount as an example of open morality; but it is evident that this is secondary to his view, while the *élan vital* is primary. He speaks as an outsider or observer in relation to the Christian mystics, while Pascal is a Christian mystic. The Christian mystic, according to Bergson receives his inspiration from the *élan vital*, while to Pascal we commune with God only through Jesus Christ. Accordingly, Bergson makes no significant contribution to the Christian faith. His contribution must be viewed in the light of his insistence upon intuition as a way of knowing reality in itself, and his emphasis upon the inner life as the seat of supra-rational knowledge. It is at this point that he draws nearest to Pascal. It is apparent that if Bergson had only followed his heart instead of his method he would have made a greater contribution to the problem of faith and reason. If he were accurate in presenting the message of the Christian mystic his affinity with Pascal would be much closer. However, when we are done with the Bergsonian conception of faith we are unsatisfied, but we do feel that his intentions are good and that he points us in the right direction. We are grateful to him for suggesting that the Christian mystics are the greatest, but we find it best to go directly to them ourselves; for this reason we turn to Pascal.

There is no doubt that Pascal's faith is deeper than that of Bergson or James, for his faith includes the good in theirs and more. He knows all they know by intuition plus what God reveals to him and while they study other mystics, Pascal has personal acquaintance with the mystic experience. Pascal knows whereof he

## FAITH AND REASON

speaks and can witness with authority to the value of this experience in his personal life and, for this reason, he is qualified to recommend it to others. We observe that the wager of James is limited by his pragmatic theory; while Pascal's wager is concerned with the existence of God and the gain of eternal life. James urges us to take a chance completely upon possibility; while Pascal urges the unbeliever to take a chance upon a God he knows to exist. This makes Pascal's argument more effective; for he can point out that our finite loss is nothing when compared with an eternal gain, being certain that God is and that He offers eternal life to those who believe in Him. Pascal feels God in his own heart and his affirmation of faith may be summed up, "I know whom I have believed and I am sure that he is able to guard until that Day what has been entrusted to me."[52]

Pascal, Bergson and James contribute a faith beyond discursive reason and one which is based upon "reasons of the heart." Faith is defined as supra-rational knowledge. Theirs is a faith seeking to know.

# FOOTNOTES AND REFERENCES

## PREFACE

1. See R. G. Collingwood, *An Essay on Philosophical Method*, 1933, Chapter III, pp. 54-91.

## CHAPTER I

1. See Pascal, Pensées, 684. The *Pensées* used in this study were translated by the present writer from F.S. Stewart's *Apology of Religion* unless otherwise designated by an asterisk (*) which indicates that they were taken from Chevalier's *Pensées De Pascal*. The numbering is that of Brunschvicg. The Appendix (pp. 97-98) presents a table which compares the numbering of Stewart with that of Brunschvicg and gives the page reference in Chevalier where the respective thought is to be found.
2. See G.M. Patrick, *Pascal and Kierkegaard*, 1947, Vol. I. pp. 108-109.
3. See *Ibid.*, p. 109. — According to Patrick the word "geometry" was used, not only for the purely spatial aspect of mathematics, but also in the generic sense, subsuming mechanics (the science of movement) and arithmetic (the science of numbers) as well as geometry in the sense now current.
4. For a more comprehensive view of Plato's world of ideas see — *Cratylus* 390 E; *Phileb.* 16 C; *Soph.* 253 B; *Theaet.* 184 C; J.A. Stewart, *Plato's Doctrine of Ideas;* A.E. Taylor, *Plato: The Man and His Work;* and Ross, *Plato's Theory of Knowledge.*
5. See *Pensées*, 460.
6. See Patrick, *op.cit.*, p. 110; cf. *Pensées*, 61.
7. See Patrick, *op.cit.*, p. 113. He bases his judgment upon Chevalier's *Conclusion of Treatises on Equilibrium of Fluids and the Weight of the Mass of Air*, p. 241.
8. See Patrick, *op.cit.*, p. 113. Here he refers to Chevalier's *Letter to Father Noel.*
9. See Patrick, *op.cit.*, p. 114. To substantiate his observation he uses Chevalier's *De L'esprit geometrique*, Chap. I, Sect. iii.
10. Cf. *Pensées*, 394.
11. See Patrick, *op.cit.*, pp. 114-115.
12. See *Ibid.* Here Patrick refers to Brunschvicg's *Genee de*

*Pascal*, p. 56ff. and Chevalier's statement, *op.cit.*, pp. 367, 368, 374, 375.
13. See *Pensées*, 72.
14. See *Ibid.*, 233; Cf. below, Chap. II, Sect. A.
15. See *Pensées*, 144.
16. See *Ibid.*, 466.
17. See *Ibid.*, 63.
18. See *Ibid.*, 65.
19. See *Ibid.*, 411.
20. See *Ibid.*, 305.
21. See *Ibid.*
22. See *Ibid.*, 556.
23. See *Ibid.*, 277, 278, 279; Cf. below, Chap. II, Sect. A.
24. Cf. Patrick, *op.cit.*, p. 125.
25. Cf. *Ibid.*, p. 126; See also *Pensées*, 278, 567, 460, 793.
26. See *Pensées*, 72.
27. See *Ibid.*
28. See *Ibid.*
29. See *Ibid.*
30. See *Ibid.*
31. See *Ibid.*
32. See *Ibid.*; Cf. Bergson, *Matter and Memory*, pp. 233-238; *Mind-Energy*, Chap. II.
33. See *Pensées*, 267.
34. See *Ibid.*, 231.
35. See Dorothy Eastwood, *The Revival of Pascal*, 1936, Chap. IV, pp. 37-47.
36. See Chevalier, "William James et Bergson," *Harvard Et La France*, e.t., n.d., p. 106 ff. (e.t. — tr. by present writer).
37. See *Ibid.*
38. H. Bergson, *Matter and Memory*, 1912, pp. xiii, 297, 293, 295, 296, 120, 121.
39. See Chevalier, *op.cit.*, pp. 112-115.
40. See C. Péquy, *Note Sur M. Bergson et la Philosophie Bergsonienne*, (e.t.), 1935, pp. 21-23.
41. See *Ibid.*, p. 47.
42. See James, *Pluralistic Universe*, 1909, p. 227.
43. See Th. Flournoy, *The Philosophy of William James*, 1917, pp. 19, 21.
44. See *Ibid.*, p. 21. Here Flournoy calls our attention to an article written by James, "Louis Agassiz," *(Memories and Studies)*, 1911.
45. Cf. James, *Pluralistic Universe*, p. 330 ff.
46. See Flournoy, *op.cit.*, p. 29.
47. Cf. *Ibid.*, pp. 32-33.

48. Cf. James, *Some Problems of Philosophy*, 1919, p. 165; See also "*Reponse Aux Remarques De M. Renouvier Sur Sa Theorie De La Volonte,*" 1888. The latter may be found in James' *Collected Essays and Reviews*, 1920, edited by R.B. Perry.

49. Cf. James, "Bradley or Bergson?" *Journal of Philosophy, Psychology and Scientific Methods*, Vol. VII, no. 2, 1910, pp. 29-33; See also James, *Collected Essays and Reviews*, pp. 333 ff., 491 ff.

50. Flournoy, *op.cit.*, p. 43.
51. Paul Tillich, *Systematic Theology*, 1951, Vol. I, pp. 42-43.
52. See James, *Some Problems of Philosophy*, pp. 5 ff., 31.
53. See *Ibid.*, p. 16.
54. See *Ibid.*, pp. 36-37.
55. See *Ibid.*, pp. 221, 222.
56. See *Ibid.*, p. 223.
57. See *Ibid.*
58. Cf. Josiah Royce, *The World and the Individual*, 1891, p. 204.
59. F.R. Bradley, *Appearance and Reality*, 1891, p. 204.
60. James, *Pragmatism*, 1908, pp. 29-31.
61. See *Ibid.*, p. 20.
62. Chevalier, "William James et Bergson," *op.cit.*, pp. 109-110; cf. Perry, *The Thought and Character of William James*, 1935, pp. 407, 422, 426-430.
63. See Eastwood, *op.cit.*, p. 80.

## CHAPTER II

1. See *Pensées*, 277.
2. See *Ibid.*, 388; cf. Eastwood, *op.cit.*, p. 25.
3. See *Pensées*, 268; cf. Ibid., 269, 267, 270, 272.
4. See *Ibid.*, 278.
5. See M. Tollemache, *French Jansensists* (n.d.), p. 193; cf. Patrick, *op.cit.*, p. 193.
6. See *Psalm*, 119, vv. 2, 7, 10, 11, 32, 34, 36, 69, 70, 80, 111, 112, 145, 161.
7. See Chevalier, *Pascal*, pp. 269-273.
8. See *Pensées*, 5.
9. See *Ibid.*, 277.
10. See *Ibid.*, 556.
11. See Jn. 17:3, (Bible quotations of the N.T. are from the R.S.V.).
12. See *Ibid.*, 1:17.
13. See *Pensées*, 556.
14. See *Ibid.*
15. See *Ibid.*, cf. Matt. 11:27.

16. See *Pensées*, 556; cf. *Ibid.*, 317, 142, 225.
17. See *Pensées*, 556; cf. 684.
18. See *Ibid.*, 684; cf. 547, 556.
19. See *Ibid.*, 549; cf. 548, 547, 785; cf. Brunner, *The Mediator*, (n.d.), p. 172; here Brunner calls the Bible the "crib of Christ"; See also *Ibid.*, p. 13 ff.
20. See *Pensées*, 284; cf. *Ibid.*, 286, 287.
21. See *Ibid.*, 288.
22. See *Ibid.*, 599.
23. See *Ibid.*, 230.
24. See *Ibid.*, 233.
25. See *Ibid.*, — The underlining is mine for stress. For a discussion on this statement see below Chap. III, Sect. D.
26. See *Ibid.*, 233, 234.
27. See Chevalier, *Pascal*, p. 241 f.; cf. *Pensées*, 195.
28. See *Pensées*, 233.
29. See *Ibid*.
30. See below Chap. III, Sect. D.
31. See Bergson, *Creative Evolution*, p. 139.
32. See *Ibid.*, pp. 140, 173.
33. See *Ibid.*, pp. 173, 176.
34. See *Ibid.*, pp. 177, 178.
35. See Eastwood, *op.cit.*, p. 35.
36. See *Ibid.*, pp. 38-39; cf. Bergson, *Creative Mind*, p. 306 ff.; *Introduction to Metaphysics*, p. 1 f.
37. See Eastwood, *op.cit.*, pp. 40, 44 ff.
38. I prefer to use the French *morale* instead of the English "morality" because the French word conveys the author's meaning best. It is a more comprehensive and spiritual term than the English.
39. See Bergson, *The Two Sources of Morality and Religion*, (tr. by R.A. Audra, C. Brereton and W. Carter, 1935), pp. 24-28.
40. See *Ibid.*, p. 202.
41. See *Ibid.*, pp. 209-210.
42. See *Ibid.*, pp. 35-36 — The new emotion is identified with the *élan vital* and is described, by Bergson, as an emotion surging forth from the depths of reality and making contact with the inmost being of the mystic.
43. See Bergson, *op.cit.*, pp. 37-38.
44. See *Ibid.*, pp. 40-41.
45. See *Ibid.*, p. 51.
46. See *Ibid.*, pp. 55-56.
47. See *Ibid.*, p. 60.
48. See *Ibid.*, p. 90.
49. See *Ibid.*, pp. 250-259.
50. See *Ibid.*, pp. 202-203. Bergson mentions in this passage

# FOOTNOTES AND REFERENCES

the God who reveals Himself and adds that He illuminates and warms privileged souls with His Presence. For a discussion on this see below, Chap. III, B, E.

51. Cf. Isa. 6.
52. See Bergson, *Two Sources*, pp. 219-220.
53. See *Ibid.*, pp. 221-223.
54. See *Ibid.*, pp. 227-228.
55. See *Ibid.*, p. 228.
56. See *Ibid.*, p. 229.
57. See *Ibid.*, cf. James, *The Will To Believe*, 1898, pp. 118-120.
58. See Bergson, *Two Sources*, pp. 243, 241.
59. See below Chap. III, B, C.
60. See James, *Principles of Psychology*, Vol. I, p. 259.
61. See *Ibid.*, Vol. I, pp. 239, 237, 236.
62. See *Ibid.*, Vol. I, pp. 333-334, 298, 336.
63. See *Ibid.*, Vol. I, pp. 336 ff., 343, 212.
64. See R.B. Perry, *Present Philosophical Tendencies*, 1912, p. 232.
65. See James, *Pluralistic Universe*, pp. 249-252.
66. See Emile Boutroux, "William James et l'experience religieuse," *The Philosophical Review*, Vol. XVII, 1908, p. 289; cf. J.B. Pratt, "The Religious Philosophy of William James," *The Hibbert Journal*, Vol. X, 1911-12, p. 225 ff.
67. See Pratt, *op.cit.*, p. 229.
68. See James. *The Will To Believe*, p. 1 ff.
69. See James, *Principles of Psychology*, Vol. II, p. 321.
70. See James, *Varieties of Religious Experience*, 1902, p. 53.
71. See *Ibid.*, p. 58.
72. See *Ibid.*, p. 246.
73. See *Ibid.*, p. 247.
74. See *Ibid.*, pp. 380-381, 485-486.
75. See *Ibid.*, p. 312 ff.
76. See *Ibid.*, pp. 512-513.
77. See *Ibid.*, pp. 515-517; cf. James, *The Will To Believe*, pp. 111-144.
78. See James, *Varieties of Religious Experience*, p. 519.
79. See James, *Pluralistic Universe*, p. 307.
80. See *Ibid.*, p. 308.
81. See *Ibid.*, pp. 311, 318.
82. See James, *Pragmatism*, pp. 283-285.
83. See *Ibid.*, p. 289.
84. See *Ibid.*, p. 297.
85. See *Ibid.*, p. 298.
86. See James, *The Meaning of Truth*, 1909, p. 22; cf. *Pragmatism*, p. 301.

87. See James, *The Will To Believe*, p. 11.
88. See *Ibid.*, p. 17.
89. See *Ibid.*, pp. 23-24, 25.
90. See *Ibid.*, p. 26.
91. See *Ibid.*, pp. 27-28.
92. See *Ibid.*, pp. 29-30.
93. See *Ibid.*, pp. 58, 54-55; cf. Mark 9:40.
94. See *Ibid.*, p. 61.
95. See *Ibid.*, pp. 175-176, 181-182.
96. See James, *Some Problems of Philosophy*, 1919, p. 225.
97. See *Ibid.*, p. 227.
98. See *Ibid.*, p. 230. The italics are mine for emphasis.

## CHAPTER III

1. See Col. 1:9.
2. See above Chap. I, Sect. A.
3. See *Ibid.*, Sect. B.
4. See *Ibid.*, Sect. C.
5. See P. Tillich, *Systematic Theology*, Vol. I, p. 77; cf. *Pensées*, 277 and above Chap. II, Sect. A.
6. See above, Chap. II, A.
7. See O.W. Wright, *The Thoughts, Letters and Opuscules of Blaise Pascal*, 1861, p. 40.
8. See A. Vinet, *Studies on Pascal*, 1859, p. 230 ff. where he uses as his source M.V. Cousin's *Essay on the Truth of Pascal*, Chap. X, pp. 248-292.
9. See W. Clark, *Pascal and the Port Royalists*, 1902, p. 226.
10. See Perry, *Present Philosophical Tendencies*, pp. 231, 232.
11. See Perry, *op.cit.*, p. 234.
12. See *Ibid.*, pp. 239-240.
13. See James, *The Meaning of Truth*, pp. 42, 230; cf. *Some Problems of Philosophy*, pp. 101-102; *Pluralistic Universe*, pp. 339-340. James considers reality as more than the conceptual order, but not as distinct from the conceptual order.
14. See Perry, *op.cit.*, p. 231 ff.
15. See *Ibid.*, pp. 246-247, 248.
16. See James, *Pluralistic Universe*, Chap. VI; cf. *Ibid.*, note 1, p. 338 ff.
17. See *Ibid.*, p. 240.
18. See *Ibid.*, cf. Flournoy, *op.cit.*, p. 198 ff., and W.B. Pitkin, "James and Bergson," The *Journal of Philosophy, Psychology and Scientific Methods*, Vol. VII, 1910, p. 225 ff. for a more comprehensive study of the relationship of the thought of Bergson and James.

19. See Bergson, *Introduction to Metaphysics*, 1912, p. 1.
20. See *Pensées*, 282.
21. See *Ibid.*, 278.
22. See Eastwood, *op.cit.*, p. 166 ff.
23. See *Ibid.*, pp. 181-182.
24. See Bergson, *Two Sources*, pp. 219-220.
25. See *Ibid.*, p. 241.
26. See Eastwood, *op.cit.*, p. 44 ff.
27. See Berdyaev, *Freedom and the Spirit*, 1948, pp. 247-248.
28. See *Pensées*, 489.
29. See J. Maritain, *Ransoming the Time*, (tr. by H.L. Binesse), 1941, p. 90; cf. *Ibid.*, p. 85 ff.
30. See *op.cit.*, p. 100; cf. Chevalier, *Pensées De Pascal*, pp. xxi-xxii.
31. See Bergson, *Two Sources*, p. 256; cf. *Pensées*, 242.
32. See *Pensées*, 242.
33. See Chevalier, "William James et Bergson," *op.cit.*, pp. 114-115; cf. Maritain, *Ransoming the Time*, p. 107, and *Degrees of Knowledge*, 1937, pp. 354, 355, 305.
34. See Eastwood, *op.cit.*, pp. 173-174.
35. See *Ibid.*, pp. 171 ff.
36. See *Ibid.*, pp. 120-121.
37. See *Ibid.*, p. 170.
38. See J.B. Pratt, "The Religious Philosophy of William James," *op.cit.*, p. 232.
39. See *Ibid.*, pp. 233-234.
40. See *Pensées*, 242.
41. See Patrick, *op.cit.*, p. 154.
42. See Eastwood, *op.cit.*, pp. 81-82.
43. See James, *The Will To Believe*, p. 58.
44. See *Ibid.*, Chap. I, p. 3 ff.
45. See Eastwood, *op.cit.*, p. 84.
46. See Heb. 11:6.
47. See E. Caillet, *The Clue to Pascal*, 1943, pp. 128-129; cf. *Ibid.*, p. 127 where Caillet suggests that Pascal probably based his wager on the Bible (Deut. 30:19) and Patrick, *op.cit.*, p. 158.
48. See James, *Some Problems of Philosophy*, pp. 221-231.
49. See *Ibid.*
50. See James, *The Meaning of Truth*, Chap. X, p. 231 ff.
51. See E. Brunner, *Our Faith*, 1936, pp. 2-3, 6, 92.
52. See II Tim. 1:12.

# BIBLIOGRAPHY

### A. Primary Sources

Bergson, Henri, *The Creative Mind*, (tr. by M.L. Andison), New York: Philosophical Library, 1946.
———, *Two Sources of Morality and Religion*, (tr. by R.A. Audra, C. Brereton, W.H. Carter), New York: Henry Holt, 1935.
———, *Creative Evolution*, (tr. by A. Mitchell), New York. Henry Holt, 1911.
———, *An Introduction to Metaphysics*, (tr. by T.E. Hulme), London: G.P. Putnam's Sons, 1912.
———, *Matter and Memory*, (tr. by N.M. Paul and W.S. Palmer), London: George Allen, 1912.
———, *Mind-Energy*, (tr. by H.W. Carr), New York: Henry Holt, 1920.
———, *Time and Free Will*, (tr. by F.L. Pogson), London: George Allen, 1912.
James, William, *A Pluralistic Universe*, London: Longman's Green, 1909.
———, *Collected Essays and Reviews*, (ed. by R.B. Perry), London: Longman's, Green, 1920.
———, *Varieties of Religious Experience*, New York: Longman's, Green, 1925.
———, *The Principles of Psychology*, 2 Vols., New York: Henry Holt, 1896.
———, *Pragmatism*, New York: Longman's, Green, 1908.
———, *Some Problems in Philosophy*, New York: Longman's, Green, 1919.
———, *The Meaning of Truth*, London: Longman's, Green, 1909.
———, *The Will to Believe*, New York: Longman's, Green, 1898.
Pascal, Blaise, *Pensées De Pascal*, (ed. by J. Chevalier), Paris: Boivin, n.d.
———, *Pascal's Pensées* (tr. by H.F. Stewart), New York: Pantheon Books, Inc., 1950.
———, *Pascal's Apology for Religion*, (extracted from *Pensées* by H.F. Stewart), Cambridge: University Press, 1942.
———, *Thoughts*, (ed. by A. Molinier and tr. by C.K. Paul), London: George Bell and Sons, 1889.

———, *Pensées*, (ed. by F. Strowski), Paris: Societe Libraire Ollendorff, (n.d.).
———, *Pensées De Pascal*, (ed. by C. Louandre), Paris: Chapentier, 1854.
———, *The Provincial Letters*, (tr. by T. McCrie), New York: Robert Carter and Brothers, 1850.

## B. SECONDARY SOURCES

Augustine, Aurelius, (tr. by M. Dods) Vol. III, Edinburgh: T and T Clark, 1837.
Baldwin, J.M., *Fragments in Philosophy and Science*. New York: Charles Scribner's, 1902.
*Dictionary of Philosophy and Psychology*, 3vv., edited by J.M. Baldwin, New York: Macmillan, 1901-1902.
Berdyaev, Nicolos, *Freedom and the Spirit*. 4th ed., London: Geoffrey Bless: The Centenary Press, 1948.
Bixler, J.S., *Religion in the Philosophy of William James*, Boston: Mashall Jones, 1926.
Boutroux, Emile, "William James et l'experience religieuse," *The Philosophical Review*, Vol. XVII, (1908), p. 289 ff.
Bradley, F.H., *Appearance and Reality*, New York: Macmillan. 1893.
Caillet, Emile, *The Clue to Pascal*, Philadelphia: The Westminister Press, 1943.
Chevalier, J., "William James et Bergson," *Harvard Et La France*, (n.d.), pp. 103-121.
Clark, W., *Pascal and the Port Royalists*, New York: Charles Scribner's, 1902.
Eastwood, Dorothy M., *The Revival of Pascal*, Oxford: Clarendon Press, 1936.
Flournoy, T., *The Philosophy of William James*, New York: Henry Holt, 1917.
Hocking, W.E., *The Meaning of God in Human Experience*, New Haven: Yale University Press, 1912.
James, Wm., "Bradley or Bergson?" *Journal of Philosophy, Psychology and Scientific Methods*, Vol. VII, no. 2, (1910), pp. 29-33.
Locke, John, *An Essay Concerning Human Understanding*, 2 vols., London: T. Longman, 1796.
Marcel, Gabriel, *The Mystery of Being*, 2 vols., Vol. I, London: Harvill Press, 1950; Vol. II, Chicago: Henry Regnery, 1951.
Maritain, Jacques, *The Degree of Knowledge*, London: Geoffrey Bless, The Centenary Press, 1937.
———, *A Preface to Metaphysics*, New York: Sheed and Ward, 1939.

# BIBLIOGRAPHY

———, *Ransoming the Time*, (tr. by H.L. Binsse), New York: Charles Scribner's Sons, 1941.
Miller, L.H., *Bergson and Religion*, New York: Henry Holt, 1916.
Moore, A.W., *Pragmatism and Its Critics*, Chicago: University Press, 1910.
Moore, J.M., *Theories of Religious Experience*, New York: Round Table Press, Inc., 1938.
Oman, John, *The Problem of Faith and Freedom*, New York: A. C. Armstrong and Son, 1906.
Patrick, D.G.M., *Pascal and Kierkegaard*, 2 vols., London: Lutterworth Press, 1947.
Perry, R.B., *Present Philosophical Tendencies*, New York: Longman's, Green, 1912.
———, *The Thought and Character of William James*, 2 vols. Boston: Little, Brown, 1935, 1936.
Pitkin, W.B., "James and Bergson" *The Journal of Philosophy, Psychology and Scientific Methods*, Vol. VII, 1910, p. 225 ff.
Pratt, J.B., "The Religious Philosophy of William James," *The Hibbert Journal*, Vol. X, (1911-12), p. 225 ff.
Ross, David, *Plato's Theory of Ideas*, Oxford: The Clarendon Press, 1951.
Royce, Josiah, *The World and the Individual*, New York: Macmillan, 1900-01.
———, *Philosophy of Loyalty*, New York: Macmillan, 1908.
———, *Religious Aspect of Philosophy*, New York: Houghton, Mifflin, 1892.
Smith, Norman Kemp, *A Commentary to Kant's 'Critique of Pure Reason,'* London: Macmillan and Co., 1918.
Spencer, Herbert, *The Principles of Psychology*, Vol. I, New York: D. Appelton, 1871.
Stewart, H.F., *The Holiness of Pascal*, Cambridge: University Press, 1915.
Tennant, F.R., *The Nature of Belief*, London: The Centenary Press, 1943.
———, *Philosophical-Theology*, 2 vols., Cambridge: University Press, 1937.
Tillich, Paul, *Systematic Theology*, Vol. I, Chicago: University Press, 1951.
Tulloch. T., *Pascal*, Philadelphia: J.B. Lippincott, (n.d.).
Vinet, A., *Studies on Pascal*, Edinburgh: T & T Clark, 1859.
Wace, Henry, *The Foundation of Faith*, London: Pickering, 1880.
Ward, James, *Essays in Philosophy*, Cambridge: University Press, 1927.
———, *The Realm of Ends*, Cambridge: University Press, 1912.

# APPENDIX

The table below compares the numbering of Stewart in his *Apology of Religion*, (1942), which is an extract from the *Pensées* and the page numbers of Chevalier's with the Leon Brunschvicg's own numbering of the *Pensées* in (Granss Ecrivains de la France, et minor chez Hachette). Chevalier's work is entitled, *Pensées De Pascal*.

| Brunschvicg | Chevalier | Stewart |
|---|---|---|
| 5 | 19 | 20 |
| 61 | 34 | 27 |
| *63 | 39n. | 38 |
| 55 | 40 | 38 |
| 72 | 42 | 41 |
| 142 | 115 | 109 |
| 144 | 40 | 40 |
| 195 | 174 | 197 |
| 225 | 193 | 207 |
| 230 | 257 | 199 |
| 231 | 256 | 200 |
| 233 | 259 | 210 |
| 234 | 267 | 211 |
| 242 | 195 | 234 |
| 267 | 272 | 43 |
| 268 | 271 | 645 |
| 269 | 272 | 246 |
| 270 | 272 | 647 |
| 272 | 272 | 648 |
| 277 | 278 | 607 |
| 278 | 280 | 608 |
| 279 | 280 | 609 |
| 282 | 278 | 610 |
| 284 | 549 | 611 |
| 286 | 550 | 612 |
| 287 | 550-551 | 613 |
| 288 | 551 | 622 |
| *305 | 155 | |

| Brunschvicg | Chevalier | Stewart |
|---|---|---|
| *317 | 160 | |
| 388 | 206 | 644 |
| 394 | 210 | 267 |
| 411 | 146 | 160 |
| 460 | 460 | 243 |
| 466 | 460 | 265 |
| 489 | 239 | 347 |
| 547 | 477 | 526 |
| 548 | 476 | 568 |
| 549 | 476 | 569 |
| 556 | 476 | 11 |
| 566 | 384 | 507 |
| 567 | 521 | 600 |
| 599 | 215 | 290 |
| 684 | 368 | 503 |
| 785 | 478 | 545 |
| 793 | 543 | 549 |